Newlyn at War 1939-1945

Edited by Pam Lomax

Gwithyas Krovskrifenn Lulyn

Published by the Newlyn Archive

First published in 2010.
Republished with minor alterations in 2018
by
Newlyn Archive
The Admiralty Boathouse
23 The Strand
Newlyn TR18 5HL

archiveatnewlyn@gmail.com
http://newlynarchive.org.uk/

ISBN 978 0 9567528 0 2

This book is printed on paper which is certified by the Forest Stewardship Council as originating from sustainable sources. It is Elemental Chlorine Free, recyclable and biodegradable.

Designed by Pamela Lomax
Printed by Headland Printers

FRONT COVER IMAGE
A mine being detonated at sea. Henry Nicholas Peake served on minesweeper *HMS Fry* and the photograph comes from the family collection.
Source, Glenys Peake

BACK COVER IMAGE
PZ182 Asthore, with crew, wives and children, and the Western Union Fleet in Mounts Bay, 1947.
Source, John Foster Tonkin

CONTENTS

ACKNOWLEDGEMENTS

The authors of this book are Friends of the Newlyn Archive. Bob Harrison, George Hoare, John Cecil Jenkin, and John Foster Tonkin have written papers specifically for this publication. Their original papers are in the archive and the content has been used in different sections as appropriate. Bob Harrison is responsible for the Appendix about Newlyn War Casualties and he has also put in context Geoffrey Garnier's papers about the Home Guard, which were donated to the archive by Pat Garnier. George Hoare has recalled living in the Fradgan as a boy and has provided many of the photographs used in the book, some of which were taken by his grandfather George Curnow who was an amateur photographer. John Cecil Jenkin, living in the Coombe during the war, has written about social aspects of life in Newlyn. We have also drawn on his published writings, particularly the research he undertook about the Belgian refugees at Newlyn. John Foster Tonkin whose family lived at Treneglos Terrace, Tolcarne during the war writes about accompanying his mother to the faraway places where his father's requisitioned fishing boat was stationed and also provides insights into the life of these men who accompanied their boats to distant ports. George Barnes (who lived at Lariggan) and Ruth Richards (who lived at New Road) have also provided the archive with written accounts of their life as children during the war.

Many of the photographs come from Billy Stevenson's collection and some of the stories come from his permanent Exhibition about Newlyn that is housed in the Board School. The publication has also drawn on Billy's autobiography, which was edited by Margaret Perry and published in 2001. Margaret has donated a collection of documents about the Belgian refugees to the archive, which she put together from an extended correspondence with the child refugee Jozef Couwyzer and these have been most pertinent to this book.

We are grateful to DT Matthews for the information that he has provided about John Henry Matthews, the French Consular Agent in Newlyn during the war, which includes a handwritten biography by his father Charles D Matthews and a video interview with the latter.

The *Newlyn at War* Open Day generated a great deal of material that we have used in this book, particularly the taped group conversations that were recorded during the Open Day. These are supplemented by the conversations at the archive on a Friday morning, which are noted by Pam Lomax, and the extensive interviews conducted by Ron Hogg. Foremost amongst the people who have contributed their knowledge in this way is Raymond Peake, who has also kindly read and corrected sections of the book.

Insights about the war come from Giles Coinchein, Liz Harman, Linda Holmes, Ann Pilcher, Adrian Nicholas, Harvey Richards, Roberta St Claire, Alan Shears, Jeff Simons, Charles Symons, Sheila Thomas, Raymond Tonkin and Mary Warren.

The photographs in the book come from Josef Couwyzer, Pat Garnier, Bob Harrison, George Hoare, Linda Holmes, DT Matthews, H Matthews, Glenys Peake, Raymond Peake, Pat Pilkerton, Ruth Richards, Roberta St Claire, June Shears, Billy Stevenson, John Foster Tonkin, Raymond Tonkin, Adrian Nicholas and Douglas Williams.

References to other published work and to the online resources are listed in the footnotes. Finally, many thanks to all those people not mentioned for their help and support and to Mary Ellery, Bob Harrison, George Hoare, Ron Hogg, Cecil Jenkin, Raymond Peake, Mike Richards, Jeff Simons, Billy Stevenson and John Foster Tonkin for reading and commenting on the first draft and to Helen Burnham, Richard Cockram and Ron Hogg for proof-reading the second draft.

Introduction

On June 28 2010, the Newlyn Archive held an Open Day, *Newlyn at War*. The date was carefully chosen to coincide with the celebration of that day in 1940 when the first of the French fishing boats to leave the Ile de Sein to join the free French resistance arrived in Newlyn. Many boats followed bringing refugees to Newlyn and other fishing villages on the Cornish coast.

The French were not the first to arrive at Newlyn during the war. Fishing boats from Belgium had already sought refuge, carrying their extended families who eventually found homes in houses previously marked for demolition, while the men folk took over the fishing previously done by the Newlyn boats requisitioned by the Navy.

Newlyn and the surrounding farms and villages also became home to the hundreds of child evacuees that fled the bombs falling on the larger urban cities of England. They came in trainloads to Penzance station where they were dispersed to the families that agreed to care for them.

At Newlyn, there were many changes. Able-bodied men were drafted into the Army, Navy or Air Force; fishermen with their boats were sent to other parts of the Country for war work. The men that remained at home became local defence volunteers or were involved in clandestine operations.

Women, as usual, were indispensable to the war effort – managing their own and other children, opening their homes to refugees and the personnel from the naval base at Newlyn, working in the fields or making camouflage nets and other items no longer available because of the war.

Newlyn was physically affected. The harbour was out of bounds to villagers unless they had a pass. There was barbed wire cutting off the beaches. The beautiful iron railings were removed from outside the houses. Shelters were built to which people fled when the sirens rang out.

Like other parts of the Country, Newlyn was stripped of its ironwork, changing the appearance of streets. The pictures above show New Road, one taken in 1915 by George Curnow showing the railings in front of the houses (left), and one taken in 2004 by George Hoare with the railings removed (right). Source, George Hoare

Social Life[1]

The war resulted in fundamental changes to life in Newlyn that affected all sectors of the community, yet the general consensus suggests that these changes happened gradually with people adapting to them almost unconsciously. According to Cecil Jenkin, church and chapels continued to be full every Sunday morning and evening. They always were in the 1930s, but the war gave an extra boost as The Almighty was asked to add His influence to hoped-for victory.

Sunday Schools continued as usual although the annual outings to Carbis Bay were ceased as petrol supplies were limited to the military or essential journeys. Since few people had cars, this had little direct impact on their travel. They continued to walk or use public transport.

Mothers socialised in the afternoons at the Methodist *Bright Hour* and the *Mothers' Union* at St Peter's, adding the knitting of scarves, gloves and balaclava helmets for the Forces to their usual activities. Youth groups, Scouts and Guides carried on and as the war progressed, they all undertook various voluntary

---

[1] This section is based on J Cecil Jenkin's paper *Newlyn's Wartime Social Life*, NA 2248 unless stated otherwise

activities. The Sea Cadet Unit brought together many young men not previously known to each other, bringing about more contacts and a different social mix.

Inevitably, there were other more fundamental changes. Young men and some young women departed for life in the armed forces, thus leaving an age gap in the village and many unfilled vacancies in sports teams. The piers and harbour were closed to the public so angling and evening strolls stopped. The ever popular Pasty Suppers and Tea Parties almost disappeared with rationing and food shortages but concerts continued to be enjoyed.

Bill Mitchell (2nd from left) with 234 Squadron. Bill was billeted with Mrs Mary Hoare at Cressars from 1942-1944. She bred bull terriers and her dog Spike accompanied Bill to work each day. Source, George Hoare

The social scene was altered by the arrival of strangers. Navy and RAF personnel came to the harbour, soldiers were stationed in the area and wounded men stayed in the former Convalescent home (now Bolitho House) on the Western Green. The ten-year old Sheila Thomas' mum had two air-sea rescue men billeted in her spare room; they worked different shifts and so could share the bed.[2] The Belgian community had an Anglo-Belgian Club and while the elders kept their own social groups and customs, the children learned the Newlyn variety of English quickly and soon made friends with Newlyn children. Evacuees from London and Plymouth arrived in large numbers bringing new accents and customs but being English, they quickly became acclimatised.

A new social group occupied the field to the east of the Art Gallery. As part of the *Dig for Victory* campaign, this was turned into allotments. Seeds and fertilisers were supplied by the government. Here, mainly elderly men spent hours growing crops and trying to produce more potatoes and bigger onions than their neighbours. Making camouflage netting, collecting money for Spitfire fighter planes, making parcels for prisoners of war, sympathising over casualties, bartering over rations, sharing air raid shelters, fire-fighting groups and all kinds of voluntary war work brought people together. The Gaiety Cinema in The Coombe re-opened in 1938 after some years of closure and was always full, especially on Saturday evenings when queues stretched down to the bridge. Newlyn girls attended the dances at the Winter Gardens Ballroom at Wherrytown and when the American soldiers came to Penzance in 1944 the girls were greatly attracted to their smart uniforms and their access to well-stocked PX stores.

George Barnes remembers the Americans using the Pirates rugby ground for American football and baseball and being encouraged to join in:

'The great attractions were the sweets and chewing gum that was freely given away, but as an added bonus when they finished for the day, they would give away their kit - baseball bats, helmets, footballs - there weren't many of us who didn't have a trophy of some sort.'[3]

[2] Sheila Thomas, in conversation
[3] George Barnes, *Some Memories of My Childhood in and Around Newlyn during WW2*. NA 2140

Children and School

For the 8-year-old schoolboy George Barnes, September 3 1939 was a normal day. His family had a wireless, so they heard the Prime Minister, Neville Chamberlain, announce the start of the war with Germany, but it meant little to him.[4] Similarly, the even younger George Hoare was unable to grasp the enormity of what was happening. As a young pupil at Tolcarne School, he recalls:

> My day started regularly at 8am, and by 8.30, I was off to meet up with a couple of pals that lived nearby, and we made our way to school. These pals were John Williams (son of the local barber who was in the Royal Navy) and Barry Mathews who lived at No 1 Tolcarne Terrace. Our first stop was usually at Elsie Bakers the grocers for a pen'orth of apples each, with the accompanying tummy ache depending on whether we were sold cookers or eaters. Then to Mrs Gilberts who lived next door to Herbert Villa. This old lady usually kept a plentiful supply of Victory V Lozenges and if we had enough money, we pooled our resources to buy a tube between us. [5]

Many Newlyners recall the teachers at Tolcarne School, but whereas some remember Miss Paul as a kindly old lady in charge of the Infants, little Linda Hutchin[6] will never forget being caned across the knuckles for writing the letter 'n' back to front, a lesson she never forgot. As the children got older, their teachers became stricter, thus Miss Edwards in class II was more of a disciplinarian than was Miss Paul, and Miss Humphries who taught the older juniors used physical punishment (allowed in those days). Mr Prowse, an evacuee teacher, had class VI (GH thought he was the best of the lot) and Mr Arnold White taught the older children (and favoured the girls with higher marks). Leslie (Snowball) White was headmaster, remembered by some for his dexterity with the bamboo cane.

According to Cecil Jenkin[7], who lived in the Coombe during WW2, the war brought few changes in the school curriculum. There were interruptions to the school day to incorporate wartime drill, which included the proper use of gas masks and where to go and what to do in an air raid. How seriously this was taken is debatable; the boys soon discovered during gas mask drill that very rude noises could be made by blowing air through the sides. Linda Hutchin hated the rubber smell and was pleased to return her Mickey Mouse gas mask at the end of the war. There were also pleasant war-related activities, as when Barbara Harvey and her class from Tolcarne School went to the Bluebell Dell at Carne Woods to pick flowers to send to the blitzed London children.

Ruth Richards[8] at Tolcarne School remembers the early days of the war when the siren sounded and the children who lived near the school were allowed to run home to shelter. She lived at Charles Street and brought her friends home to take shelter in the cupboard under the stairs. Similar practices existed in the other schools, thus Miss Austin, writing in the Board School log book on September 27 1939, recorded an air raid practice in which the senior girls sheltered in Faugan Lane, other girls in Adit Lane and some in the Juniors' lobby.[9]

Later in the war, Morrison Shelters made of steel with a heavy steel plate on top and mesh around the sides were provided for school classrooms, and Anderson shelters were built in the school playgrounds. The one at Tolcarne School was partially underground with an arched metal roof. After it was built, the children were drilled frequently so that they would enter the shelters in an orderly manner to sit in lines on the chairs provided. Both types of shelter were named after government Ministers of the time.

When the air raid alerts became more frequent many children found them a welcome break from lessons. Even in wartime children preferred the freedom of the outdoors to school and, in the early days of the war, there were few restrictions on children's freedom to roam on the seashore and in the harbour.

Ricky 'Ticky Tavy' Clitheroe, an evacuee in Newlyn Town tells many stories of the escapades of his 'gang'. This consisted of Philip Harvey who lived just below Well Cottage and whose father was a shoemaker; Walter 'Goodey Two Shoes' Goodey who lived in Church Street and whose father was a sign maker; Neil 'Swanny' Swanson whose father was a preacher; Billy 'Roughneck' Rouffignac, who often stayed with his Nan at Sandy Cove near the South Pier and whose father was in the Navy; George Barnes whose father became the harbour pilot; and Tony Stevenson who lived at Roseland in Trewarveneth Street. On one

---

[4] Barnes NA 2140
[5] George Hoare, *Memories of Boyhood in WW2*. NA 2191
[6] Linda Holmes, in conversation
[7] Jenkin NA 2248
[8] Ruth Richards, *Memories of WW2*. NA 1948
[9] John Cecil (Chirgwin) Jenkin *Newlyn: A View from Street-an-Nowan*, 2009:72

occasion, some of the boys were swimming from Skilly beach, just below the quarry and went to investigate a mysterious object in the sea, which turned out to be a live mine. Fortunately, it was spotted by the coastguard and the lifeguard towed it out to sea where a minesweeper from Falmouth dealt with it.[10]

Billy Stevenson[11] and his friends commandeered a damaged punt that had been left on the Old Quay, full of holes that he and his friends plugged with corks. The punt was from the *Suffolk Rose*, a Lowestoft fishing boat that fished out of Newlyn; it had been attacked by E-boats and the holes were from machine gun bullets. Many of the restrictions that were imposed came from such hazards, and there were numerous posters in the town and at school warning children and adults against messing with strange objects. Despite this, George Hoare remembers the pleasure of turning rocks over at the bottom of the Coombe River in search of whatever he could find; George Barnes recollects picking up oranges and other flotsam at the tide line, no doubt discharged by one of the ships sunk in the Western Approaches. He also collected Perspex and plywood from the RAF base to make model aeroplanes or to swap with others.[12]

Several people at Newlyn remember the minesweeping trawler *Royalo* being blown up just outside Penzance harbour one Sunday morning in September 1940. The trawler was passing on the seaward side of the Gear Pole when there was a huge plume of smoke followed by an explosion. The *Royalo* was an old steam trawler that had been requisitioned by the Navy and allocated as a minesweeper to clear Mount's Bay of the mines parachuted in by the enemy. Eight survivors were rescued.[13] According to Billy Stevenson, it was a Sunday morning and the Royalo's degaussing[14] equipment had been turned off for Sunday lunch![15]

Henry N Peake served on Minesweeper HMS Fly, part of the 12th Minesweeping Flotilla, during WW2. He was awarded the DMS for outstanding courage as a result of diving onto the propeller of HMS Fly to clear away the wire of an enemy mine mooring that was fouling the propeller. Source, Glenys Peake

Once the children reached a certain age, they could join one of the military training corps organised by the services, like the Sea Cadets at Newlyn. Billy Stevenson was a Sea Scout and he and about twenty boys would be taken out in their sailing gig for training by Andrew Harvey, none of them wearing life jackets. Jim Hosking was a member of the Penzance Squadron of the Air Training Corps. He remembers being taken to Newlyn one Sunday morning in 1944 to see the Air Sea Rescue boat stationed there. He thought that these boats were almost unsinkable, self-righting and watertight, until the crewman who took the boys round told them that the rescue boat had been called out the night before and the conditions were so bad that even in their 'unsinkable' boat they had barely managed to get back.

---

[10] Richard Clitheroe, *Away from the Bombs* Dyllansow Truron 1990:38-41
[11] Margaret Perry (Ed) *Growing up with Boats: an autobiography of Billy Stevenson*, 2001:47
[12] Barnes NA2140
[13] Perry 2001:59
[14] Degaussing is to neutralize the magnetic field of (a ship) by encircling it with a conductor carrying electric currents
[15] Billy Stevenson, in conversation

Red Cross detachment 1941. Source, Linda Holmes

A Woman's Lot

Many young single women volunteered and joined the Women's Royal Naval Services (WRENS) the Auxiliary Territorial Service (ATS) or the Women's Auxiliary Air Force (WAAF). The women, who stayed at home while their men were engaged with war work, had to deal with home and family as well as the extra duties brought about by the war. This was not a new role for those whose husbands were fishermen, as they were used to managing the household while their husbands were at sea.

But even for these women, the changes taking place must have seemed momentous. It was 'a time when an almost continuous stream of circulars and telegrams was issued from Whitehall dealing with such diverse matters as the detention of aliens, the reception of evacuees, producing food in the back garden (digging for victory) and the removal of signposts and other means of identifying locations'.[16] Food rationing and fire precautions were organised, gas masks were issued and lights were blacked out.

George Barnes recalls:

> All streetlights were permanently extinguished, and we were instructed to black out all the windows of our house from dusk to dawn. Mother went to the West End Drapery Store in Penzance and bought a large quantity of black linen cloth, we acquired some wooden laths and we set to work making frames for each window, these were then lined with the black cloth. The only window that was not blacked out was in the small toilet at the top of the stairs; it was considered that that was a job that could be achieved without the aid of a light, and so the bulb was removed.[17]

Some women worked from home making camouflage nets. Materials were provided free and the simple tools were a hook on a wall, a small piece of wood as a template for the mesh size and a large wooden needle. Cecil Jenkin remembers helping with the task; in his house the hook on the wall hung by the kitchen slab. He remembers delivering the completed nets and returning home with the cash and further supplies of twine.[18] Sheila Thomas[19] also collected materials from the bottom of Chywoone Hill where the British Legion is now to make the nets for her mother. Sheila and her two sisters had to thread the needles before they were allowed out to play.

In 1943 all married women without small children had to work. Mrs Ruby Jenkin went to work in the kitchen at Penlee House in Penzance, then a private residence owned by the Branwell family. She also formed a fire-fighting team, with steel helmet, buckets and stirrup pump.[20]

---

[16] Phyllis M Rowe and Ivan Rabey, *Air Raid Warning Red* <bbc.co.uk/ww2peopleswar> June 17 2005
[17] Barnes NA 2140
[18] Jenkin 2009:170-188
[19] Sheila Thomas, In conversation
[20] Cecil Jenkin, A Schoolboy at War, OCS Journal 1993

Miriam Richards, who lived with her husband Leslie and three children at 12 Charles Street, wrote about wartime conditions to her sister in Boston and her letter (on the right) was published in the *Boston Evening American* in 1941.

Miriam's daughter Ruth explains:

My father was a special policeman during the war. As he went out on duty during an alert, he would see that our neighbours and we children went indoors to shelter. He did fire watching duties at night at the cable office in Penzance, an important building receiving worldwide information. The square white building is still there and has recently been converted into flats.

In her letter, Miriam Richards describes an alert:

The alert was two hours long last night, from 7pm to 9pm. Les was out all the time. Ruth goes under the stairs in the cupboard. They say that's the safest place, and I'm in there quite a number of times during the week.

Every plane that goes droning over I go in there, feeling sure it's a Jerry. Would you believe it, its five minutes since I started, and the siren has begun the most unearthly sounds, enough to turn you sick. Ruth is in the cupboard now. Les is putting on his tin hat, his gas mask is slung over his back, his whistle in his pocket. He'd rather be out than in. Joyce is down at Peggy's for tea.

Joyce Richards was seventeen years old and having tea with her friend, Peggy Teague at West Terrace. She would later serve in the WRENS. Harvey Richards was at Truro School and later served in the Royal Navy. Lillie Harvey, the milk girl came to the houses delivering milk from churns and she will be remembered by many.

Miriam refers to Sunday evening services at Trinity Chapel, which were brought forward to enable people to be at home before dusk. In her bible she kept *A Prayer for the Men at the Front* that could be sung to the tune *Eternal Father Strong to Save* and was probably sung by many in Newlyn during the war and the *Service of Thanksgiving on the Fourth Anniversary of the Outbreak of War,* which must have been September 3 1943, at Newlyn Trinity Chapel.[21]

---

[21] Richards NA1953, NA1954

This is another in a series of letters from Britishers to friends and relatives in Greater Boston.

From: 12 Charles st., Newlyn, Cornwall, England.

To: Mrs. Edith Richards, 34A Perrin st., Roxbury, Mass.

Dear Edith:

Without a doubt you will be very surprised to get a letter from me. We just had tea and have settled down for the evening, I hope. Les has just said he supposes the siren will go in a minute.

The alert was two hours long last night, from 7 p. m. to 9 p. m. Les was out all the time. Ruth goes under the stairs in the cupboard. They say that's the safest place, and I'm in there quite a number of times during the week. Every plane that goes droning over I go in there, feeling sure it's a Jerry.

Would you believe it, it's five minutes since I started and the siren has begun the most unearthly sounds, enough to turn you sick. Ruth is in the cupboard now.

PUTS ON TIN HAT

Les is putting on his tin hat, his gas mask is slung over his back, his whistle in his pocket. He'd rather be out than in.

Joyce is down at Peggy's for tea. Peggy was here the Sunday Harvey was home at mid-term. Our thoughts always go to him whenever we get an alert. He can't do as well in his work as he could in normal times, he can't concentrate.

In a couple of weeks there comes his exam for his Matric. I don't put a lot on his passing but I shall be disappointed if he fails.

Lots of people would rather hear the alert than not, they feel it quickens all military and naval servants to the enemy. Ruth is still in the cupboard. Les fetched Joyce here and has gone off again. The plane here over the harbor has been fired from the harbor. We are used to it but we will be glad when it is over and we can breathe freely again.

The Greeks have done splendidly, haven't they? I expect Mussolini feels rather small. What do you think of the way we are being left almost all alone to fight it out?

NO SERVICE NOW

There are no evening services now and I think that's best, it enables everybody to be indoors just before dark. Services start at 3:45 p. m.

The all clear has just sounded. A bare hour tonight. That's a blessing, I'm sure.

The snaps are all shown to everyone. Lillie Harvey the milk girl is always asking for more snaps. I should like to see David and kiss him a bit. Keep your tea and have an extra drink yourself, we have more than we can drink.

We have enough to spare in lots of things. You said you hoped my leg was better. It is definitely much better but not to my liking—I am still lame, or perhaps limp would sound better. I shall feel it a year or two, the doctor says. I don't mind anything if it gets better eventually.

No cleaning whatever was done this year, instead of the ceilings done twice a year. Les did the kitchen and wash house. Everything else was left to slide.

Les has gone down to his mother's. He scarcely gets a minute to sit down, what with the siren and duty.

BOMBS DROP CLOSE

He doesn't like being in the cable office. One dropped at the front of it another at the back a fortnight ago. Les was on there last Tuesday from 10 p. m. to 2 a. m.

The other duty there is 2 a. m. to 6 a. m.—then walk home, have breakfast, and go to work. It is all voluntary. You see, we are all helping to win the war. Les thinks about his father. He is nearly driven insane.

Frank came over to fetch them in the car this morning and brought them home during the alert. He was held up coming across the town about his lights. Ma is up the hill waiting.

The news is on (radio) so I will close. I'm going to bed soon. Les is still down there. Love to all from Miriam.

British Forces Occupy Tahiti

BERLIN, Jan. 18 (INS)—The official German news agency DNB reported from Hsinking today that British forces are reported to have occupied the French-owned South Seas island of Tahiti.

George Hoare's grandfather, George Curnow, was Chief Air Raid Warden in the Penzance district and he must have led a similar life to Les Richards, being on call almost continuously.

The number of shops at Newlyn diminished as a result of the men being called up and due to the shortages and rationing. Mr Edwards had a grocery shop on the corner of St Peter's Hill in Newlyn Town. There was a Co-op in Street-an-Nowan; it had an overhead tube attached to a wire in which money was sent to a cashier and the change sent back. Jelbert's ice cream parlour was in the Strand;[22] Jack Williams' barber shop nearby shut down when he joined the Navy, opening again after the war.

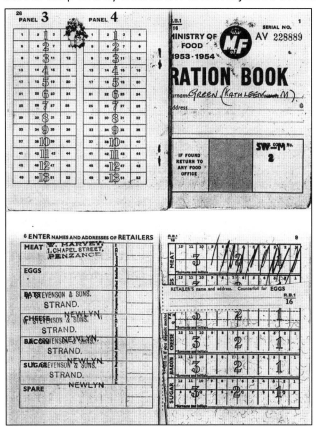

Left: Ration book of Kathleen Green with names of retailers. Source, Billy Stevenson Collection

The Stevensons had two shops: a grocers shop in the Strand, and a shop on the corner of Trewarveneth and Fore Street, known as Maud's Shop. This was just below the Stevenson bakery, which had five bakers before the war, but was reduced to one during the war.[23] Maud's was a hub of activity during the war, a place where the women met to gossip and exchange coupons. Miss Maud Thomas who lived at Primrose Terrace had stepped in to fill a gap when the previous shop girl, Phyllis Chiffers, had eloped suddenly with a fisherman. As the queue lengthened outside the shop door, Billy Rowney, in desperation, had asked for a volunteer from the fish cellar next door where Maud was one of the women packing fish. When she stepped forward, Maud could not have known that she would run the shop for the next 40 years.[24]

During the war, everything was in short supply and rationing became a way of life; ration books containing coupons were issued to everyone for clothes as well as food. Often the shops sold out, so even with coupons, it was a lottery. Women devised all sorts of ways of swapping their coupons so as to get the things they wanted most. Roberta St Claire was just two when she was evacuated. She remembers the café mornings on a Thursday when aunty and six friends would meet and swap ration book coupons. Because clothes coupons were in short supply, aunty made Roberta a coat on her hand sewing machine from an old RAF uniform; it was rough, and the child did not like it but recognised that it was made with much love.[25]

George Barnes recalls living with very basic things:

> We grew vegetables in the garden... my Uncle George was a farmer, so we were able to get potatoes and the occasional rabbit... also being that we lived close to Newlyn I was able to scrounge some fish... The meagre ration of meat was conjured by my mother to make stews and a stockpot. Occasionally we were lucky enough to get some tripe or other offal... We were lucky having a couple of apple trees in the garden plus fruit bushes; mother bottled much of the produce... We had to make shoes last... when holes appeared in the soles, I purchased a tube of Rhinosole. I re-soled our shoes, using a table knife to cover the soles with a thick layer of the compound... I serviced the shoes for my mum, grandmother, aunt, and myself.[26]

WAR TIME SPONGE

<u>Ingredients</u>
2 re-const, dried eggs.
3 tablespoonsful white sugar.
Beat these together till creamy.
<u>Add</u>
4 tablespoonsful S.R. flour.
1 teaspoonful cream of tartar.
Pinch of salt.
½ small teaspoonful Bicarbonate of Soda
 (dissolved in warm milk).
Then 3 or 4 tablespoons milk.
Divide into tins and bake in fairly hot oven for about 10 minutes (Regulo 7) filling as desired.

Source, Ruth Richards

---

[22] Where Vi's hairdressers is now
[23] Perry 2001:47
[24] Maud's closed in 1961. Billy Stevenson, in conversation
[25] Roberta St Claire, *Evacuee Aged Two*, NA 1793
[26] Barnes (NA 2140)

Evacuees from London

It was the women's work to house and care for the young evacuees that came from London and Plymouth to Newlyn, which was designated a safe area. The children and their teachers came in two waves in June 1940.[27] Schools were closed at noon and they became receiving and billeting centres. None of the schools (the Board School on Chywoone Hill, the Infant School at Trewarveneth Street and the Tolcarne School) could cope with so many new pupils, and in October, Trinity Methodist Sunday School became an overflow school with Mrs Arkwright as the Headteacher.[28]

Ricky Clitheroe, a four-year-old evacuee, remembers being 'put on charabancs with our little suitcases. Gas masks hung over our shoulders and large labels with our names and addresses on were tied to the lapels of our coats'. At Penzance station, 'we were heralded in and sat on school chairs in rows, with a mug of tea and a sandwich each... I was blowing my nose on a piece of white sheet that my mum had pinned to my shirt...'[29] Ricky was lucky in that he was billeted at Well Cottage in Newlyn Town with the childless Charlie and Liz Tresize who treated him as an adopted son. Other evacuees mentioned in his book are Dorothy and John Smith who lived below Well Cottage and Billy Wells who lived nearby at Eden Place.

The very young children often came to love their foster parents more than they did their real parents. Roberta St Claire from London was only two when she was sent to Whitby Bay and, by the end of the war, she had got to know her aunty better than she knew her mother. The older evacuees found it much harder to settle and were often a disruptive force in the schools. Not all the children's new aunties were kind, and some were positively cruel to the children they were supposed to care for.

A small evacuee aged two.
Source, Roberta St Claire

Many local children made friends with the evacuees and their friendships lasted long after the war had ended, exchanging letters and photographs. For example, Louis Ledez and his fisherman father and mother lived near to Ann Rosewall and her family at Penzance. The two young people became great friends, with the older Louis teaching Ann the French nursery melody Frère Jacques during the air raids.[30]

Left: Ellie Emily Curnow with three young evacuees at Homealong on Chywoone Hill during WW2. Source, George Hoare

Below: The family Chapman who lived at 1 Treneglos Terrace in 1941 while the Tonkin family were at Lamlash. Source, JF Tonkin

[27] Cornishman September 3 2009
[28] Jenkin 2009:71
[29] Clitheroe 1990: 3-5
[30] Ann Pilcher NA1761

Commandeered Women

Some women, whose husbands had signed up to remain with their requisitioned fishing boats, took their families to the ports to which their husbands were assigned. Phyllis Tonkin was married to John Foster Tonkin, one of the crew of *PZ18 United Boys*, which was commandeered by the Navy for service in the Western Approaches. Very early in the war, she and some of the other wives decided to follow their husbands to their postings, where they rented accommodation for themselves and their children. Phyllis and her small son who was aged three at the outset of the war travelled first to Padstow and then followed the *United Boys* to Scotland. Hers is a remarkable story, recorded in the photographs in her family album and shared with her son: [31]

At Padstow. Charlie Symons (who was on the Rosebud), with his hand on the shoulder of his wife Mary Symons (née Corin). On his left Phyllis Tonkin, Olga Mary Tonkin, wife of William Henry Tonkin and one other. Front row, L to R. John Foster Tonkin aged 3 with three other Newlyn children. Source, JF Tonkin

> Often Mother would recall the very long wartime train journey to Scotland, stopping and starting, sometimes in cuttings and tunnels when an Air Raid was imminent. I think the journey took us about two days and two nights and then we had the sea crossing from Ardrossan to Brodick on the Isle of Arran.
>
> The *United Boys* was stationed at Lamlash, close to Brodick and my parents rented a cottage, only yards from the beach, and near to the jetty, called Douglas Villa. We were there by June 1941 and I was almost four years of age. Father's sister in law, Olga Mary Tonkin (née Williams) was there with her two sons, my cousins William Henry and his brother Raymond Thomas. Both were older than I was and went to school on the Island.
>
> I just about remember the beach, playing on the sands and crossing a rickety wooden bridge to visit my cousins. Unlike Newlyn (where the harbour was a restricted area), we could go on to the short jetty and on to the *United Boys*. There I remember catching whitebait; they were so plentiful; Father would just lower a bucket over the side and then lift it slowly out of the sea.

> Photo: Walter Chiffers, his sister Phyllis Tonkin, Elizabeth T Chiffers and children JF Tonkin aged 4 and cousin Paul Chiffers aged nine months, at Douglas Villa., Lamlash, Isle of Arran. Source, JF Tonkin

The women kept in touch with folk in Newlyn while they were away. In a letter card postmarked 1941 to the evacuees, Ida, Mary and 'Dad' Chapman who lived in her house at 1 Treneglos Terrace, Newlyn, Phyllis Tonkin wrote:

> Glorious weather here ... I am writing this on the beach, the boy is down in the water with his swimming costume on. Have you used all your coupons yet? What a life Ida, how shall we manage for stockings, bare legs at the present? I hear that dear little Beauty, the bird has died but tell 'dad' not to worry as I know he has looked after him, I expect he misses him.

---

[31] John Foster Tonkin, *Newlyn's Commandeered Fishing Boats*, September 15, 2010. NA 2249

Phyllis had received a letter from her neighbour, Mrs Catherine (Aunt Katie) Williams who lived at 30 Charles Street, Newlyn, that the evacuees had killed the budgerigar. They were frying or cooking and caused so much smoke and fumes that the bird suffocated.

In another card, written about the same time, Olga Tonkin to her sister-in-law Florence Annie Tonkin at Gwavas House, Newlyn wrote:

> We received the Primus and all the other things safe, also the coat. The only thing that is scarce here is vegetables. A leek is 6d each, rhubarb 6d a lb, carrots 6d a lb. It is quiet here; there is no air raid warning here. We have heard them flying overhead in the night once or twice going on their way to Glasgow. That is all. We are very glad to have the Primus it is a big help to me. I must thank you very much.
>
> We can see the mainland from here easy, and when there are bombs being dropped over there, we can see the explosions easy, we saw them last week, it lit up the sky sometimes. We are all, all right and so is John's family. There is no harbour here, just a jetty running out for the Steamer. We are always at anchor, come ashore in the punt for everything.

Phyllis did not accompany the other families to Ireland, returning to Newlyn with her son. She did visit her husband in South Wales and she often spoke about the journey from Penzance by train. There was an Air Raid warning when she was in the vicinity of Bristol and the train was brought to a halt in the Severn railway tunnel – a frightening experience.

Fishing and War

Fishermen in the Royal Naval Reserve reported for duty in 1939. Other Newlyn men signed up. Some fishing boats were requisitioned by the Navy and their crews became Navy personnel.

In 1940, there were still enough fishing boats at Newlyn for them to report to Falmouth to take part in the Dunkirk evacuations, which took place between May 27 and June 3 1940. This was when British, French and Belgian troops cut off by the German army were evacuated from the beaches and harbour of Dunkirk. Many of the troops were carried back to Britain by a flotilla of around 700 boats, including fishing boats, whose civilian crews were called into service for the emergency.

Although Newlyn boats went to Falmouth to play their part, they were not used in the evacuation. This happened to the *PZ88 Madeline*, owned by Mr Willis; having put into Dover on the way home from the herring fishery at Lowestoft, she was requisitioned by the Navy and sent to Falmouth.[32] The Mousehole boat *PZ46 Internos,* owned by David and Eddy Sleeman was commandeered for wartime service at Falmouth but did not go to Dunkirk despite a brass plaque on the deck that said she did.[33]

Left: Prisoner of war Johnny Greengrass (centre).
Source, Billy Stevenson Collection

Johnny Greengrass from Newlyn was skipper of one of the rescue boats at Dunkirk. His ship was destroyed by shells but fortunately, he was pulled from the sea by the crew of a paddle steamer. He regained consciousness on a stretcher next to the paddles - only to see a dive-bombing German Stuka bearing down on him. The paddle steamer took a direct hit and the blast knocked Lt Greengrass unconscious; yet again, he was plunged back into the sea. Miraculously he was washed up onto the beach at Dunkirk, where allied soldiers dressed him in the dry uniform of a dead army private and left him to be rescued. Instead, he was captured by the Germans, who refused to believe he was a naval officer until his true identity was confirmed by the Red Cross.[34]

With the fear of a German invasion, a number of precautions were put in place around the country that affected Newlyn. The Immobilisation of Vehicle Order, 1940, required fishermen to ensure that the enemy could not use the boats left in the harbour, so they had to remove vital parts from the engines of motor or steam boats, and oars, rudders and masts from sailing and rowing boats. Life was difficult for those fishermen who continued to fish. They faced petrol rationing and restrictions on fishing grounds. All fishing

[32] Perry 2001:35-36
[33] Jeff Simons, in conversation
[34] Unknown newspaper cutting, Billy Stevenson Collection NA1789

boats needed a permit before they went to sea. The use of radios was banned in case the enemy intercepted the messages, although fishermen could use the radio to warn the Navy if they saw German aircraft or submarines. If a trawler was sunk, the crew would receive a month's wages.[35]

Sometimes the government would borrow motor fishing boats for a few months. The local Fishery Officer had to select the boats whose use would cause the least hardship to the owners and least affect fish supply to the country. As the war progressed, smaller boats, which included many of the Lowestoft boats (50hp engines), such as *FR242 Efficient, LT151 Boys Friend, LT711 Lord Fisher* and *YH129 Helpmate,* were sent to fish elsewhere. On March 30 1941, *YH129 Helpmate* sailed from Newlyn and disappeared with all ten hands. The skipper of *Helpmate* was called Leggett and lodged with his wife at North Corner.[36] There came a point when the only boats left working at Newlyn were *PZ51 Mayflower*, skippered by Richard 'Dicky' Worth and *PZ319 Acacia (ex Girl Lillian)*, owned and skippered by the Richards family.[37] The lack of skippers and engineers was a pressing problem and in March 1941 Fishery Officer W H Barron made a plea to the Ministry to exempt some of these men from military service:

> Apart from deck hands, the recent calling-up of fishermen includes Skippers and Engineers of fishing craft of all kinds. Unfortunately, the majority of these boats are already undermanned owing to quite a number of the younger men serving with the armed forces. In many cases where a temporary postponement of Military Service has been granted the time limit has now expired. Unless further exemption is obtained in the near future, a considerable number of boats will have to layup, as these men holding such key positions cannot be replaced. I am well aware that the men are needed for service with the forces but am of the opinion that it would be in the national interest if the utmost consideration was given to the position of the leading Skippers and Engineers of each Port with a view to securing their conditional exemption. The majority of these men do not wish to evade Military Service, but from the food production point of view it should be seriously considered whether it would not be better for them to be retained in their present positions, as there is already a serious shortage of fish in many parts of the country.[38]

Conditions at Newlyn during the war were not easy for the fishermen. The boats that were not requisitioned by the Admiralty were mainly the small pilchard drivers, which were restricted to inshore lining during daylight hours or to pilchard catching. This was not the kind of fishing that the men whose boats were requisitioned had done before the war. In 1942, Rodda Williams and Ben Batten were lost on their boat, Dashing Spray (PZ23). According to Billy Stevenson, they may have pulled one net too many and it was too much for the undecked boat to handle.[39]

Inshore fishing was dangerous because the coast was covered in barbed wire and the beaches booby-trapped. Billy Stevenson recalls:

> When fishing at night... with no ships showing lights, you would suddenly become aware of a large stern looming ahead of you. You were lucky sometimes to hear the discharge water from the engine, and then you would know a boat was there. You might get a call from someone on deck asking who was there.

> In the daytime, you would see the barrage balloons above them, these were about five hundred feet high and stopped planes diving on the ships, they would have become caught in the wires. I have seen as many as fifteen to twenty boats in Mounts Bay waiting to join a convoy to go up the English Channel.

The tosher *PZ82 Chicadee* landing Home Guard during a training exercise with the army.
Source, Billy Stevenson Collection

As a boy, in the early years of the war, Billy Stevenson fished from the small pilchard driver *PZ82 Chicadee*, named after a type of bird and once owned by the Garnier family. When no night fishing was allowed, he shot 'moored nets' from the *Chicadee* during the evening with Joe Carr and Lawrie Vingoe, and hauled them the following day. The catch provided bait for *PZ123 Mayon Castle*, and when this was not required, was sold to the

[35] *The Second World War* <HistoryShelf.org> September 23 2010
[36] Perry 2001:78
[37] McWilliams 2007:87
[38] Fishery Officer W H Barron, *Quarterly Report to the Cornwall Sea Fisheries Commission*, March 12 1941 (PRO/MAF 209/283)
[39] Perry 2001:52

market and the scads went to the Sanatogen Works in the Coombe to use as fish manure in the manufacture of farm and market garden fertiliser. In 1943, the fifteen-year-old Billy (who had left school earlier than his father wished because of the war) joined Joe Carr and the Belgians Victor Vantorre and Emil Calibut as one of the four-man crew on *PZ595 Girl Sybil*. His father had purchased this boat from Sybil Vingoe (the manageress of the Stevenson shop in the Strand) after the death of her father. Earlier in the war, the *Girl Sybil*, captained by Joe Carr, had rescued the crew of *PZ476 Margaret* after her engines caught fire and towed the boat back to Newlyn.

Newlyn Harbour

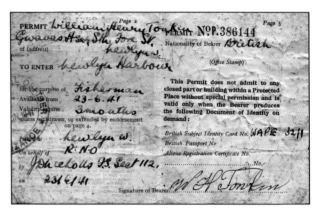

Permit for WH Tonkin b1860 to enter Newlyn Harbour, dated June 23, 1941. Source, JF Tonkin.

There were many changes to the operation of the harbour. The north and south piers were closed and there were sentries on guard. Access was by pass, which was obtained from the hut adjacent to Barron's Newsagents in the Strand. There were three machine guns at the end of the pier and a boom defence at the mouth of the pier. Boats entering the pier had to have a password that was changed nightly. The harbour clerk was Arthur (Turk) Thomas who had been invalided out of the Navy.[40]

Work at Penlee Quarry was an important part of the war effort. Many people recall the regular-as-clockwork twice-daily blasts at the quarry and the trains that pulled trucks loaded with blue elvan along the beach at Sandy Cove to the South Pier where the contents would be tipped down a large chute until the stone boat was loaded. The driver of the quarry train was Janner Maddern who lived in Roskilly Cottages.[41]

Left: Ben Hoare and Everett Kitchen who were pilots at Newlyn during the war. Source, George Hoare

It was the job of harbour pilots to escort the stone boats in and out of the harbour. The stone boats had a dangerous job, and many came to grief. Very early in the war (November 15 1939), the cargo ship *Woodtown,* with a cargo of blue elvan from Newlyn, detonated a mine off Margate and sank, killing most of the crew.[42]

Newlyn also played host to a number of different craft during WW2, like the armed trawler *Capstone* or the minesweeping trawler *Royalo*.[43] The threat from enemy planes meant that ships would wait in Mount's Bay to join outward-bound convoys and come into the harbour if they were damaged. Newlyn Harbour was a base for a detachment of RAF air sea rescue launches (ASRL); these went to the aid of aircrew who had ditched in the sea. Jimmy Peake witnessed the large black cloud that rose over the rooftops when a motor torpedo boat travelling at high speed across the bay hit two floating mines just after it passed the Low Lee buoy. Fortunately, its speed meant that it escaped the full force of the explosion and it was able to limp back to Newlyn harbour.

[40] Perry 2001:34, 65
[41] Diane Bond, in conversation with Bob Harrison
[42] Billy McGee, *They Shall Grow Not Old* (billy1963@ntlworld.com)
[43] Jenkin 2009:170-188

Left: Air Sea Rescue Launch 004 with the hulk *Cretehill* behind. Source, Billy Stevenson Collection.

The Air Force built a concrete blockhouse as living quarters for men on duty, including local men, at the end of the North Pier.[44] The building included an 'airman's ablutions' much to the amusement of the locals. Jim Harman, the fifth man from the left in the photo on the left, was billeted at 5 Carn Gwavas Terrace with Betsy Liddicot. The family introduced him to his future wife, whom he returned to marry in 1947, staying at Newlyn for the rest of his life.[45]

From 1942-1943 the ASR base at Newlyn had four pinnaces. Bill Allen served on *Pinnace 1234*. He was billeted at 16 Treneglos Terrace, where an efficient Cornish Landlady, Mrs Bickley and her husband a train driver, made him welcome. Mrs Bickley's Cornish pasties were out of this world and if the men were called out during a meal, she would stick name flags in the unfinished portions to await their return. Later (1943) Bill became part of the crew on *HSL 2554*, one of four high-speed launches that replaced the pinnaces.[46]

As well as the Air Force, the Royal Navy had a naval base at Newlyn. J Henry Matthews (the French Hon Consul) was responsible for forming a Navy choir called *Shanty Boys*. There were plenty of men for the choir because the fast naval motor launches stationed at Newlyn all had a crew of eighteen men. The launches had small hospital cabins on the aft deck, carried depth charges, had machine guns either side of the bridge and a gun on the foredeck. The St Ives artist George Fagan Bradshaw (b1887) who was in the Royal Navy during WW2 was involved in an accident when his boat triggered a magnetic mine in Newlyn Harbour. The naval headquarters was in the Harbour Offices opposite the Post Office. The man in charge was the retired Vice Admiral, Commander C H Pilcher who lived in rooms at the Newlyn Mission.[47]

Newlyn's Requisitioned Fishing Boats

During WW2 the motorised Newlyn fishing boats were commandeered for service with the Royal Navy. The captains and crews of the boats were encouraged to stay with their boats as long as they passed the medical examination for entry to the Royal Navy Reserve, which in 1940 was held at Newlyn in the offices of Stevenson and Sons.[48] In all 20 boats were commandeered.[49]

The boats were described as motor fishing vessels (MFVs), Naval Auxiliary Boats and Harbour Defence Patrol Craft. As Kite Balloon Tenders or Barrage Balloon Vessels, they would fly a barrage balloon on a length of cable and operate between other vessels as a hindrance to low flying enemy aircraft, not allowing them to come low enough to aim for a direct hit. They would take food and other stores to vessels lying off shore in deeper waters and move personnel from boat to boat or shore to boat. Some boats were used for mine watching at night, looking for parachutes dropping enemy bombs. They were the day to day 'work horses' being a small but vitally important part of the Royal Navy.

Six of the commandeered Newlyn fishing boats - *PZ182 Asthore, PZ120 Cornishman, PZ17 Peel Castle, PZ87 Rosebud, PZ214 Two Boys* and *PZ18 United Boys* - were allocated to serve on the Western side of the United Kingdom; that is to say the Bristol Channel, Irish Sea and the Firth of Clyde.[50]

Other boats were stationed nearer home; *PZ107 Renovelle* and *FY405 (later PZ84) Swift* were allocated to Penzance; *PZ46 Internos* and *PZ81 Lyonesse* went to the Harbour Service Pool at Falmouth, along with the private motor yacht, *Morwenna* which became a degaussing boat there; *PZ12 Goodwill* owned by its skipper Fred Hichens was attached to Newlyn/St Ives but released to resume fishing before the end of the

---

[44] Perry 2001:34
[45] Liz Harman, Archive Day June 28 2010
[46] Bill Allen, People's War Archive <bbc.co.uk/ww2peoples war>
[47] Jenkin 2009:170-188
[48] Perry 2001:34
[49] Billy Stevenson
[50] Tonkin, NA 2249

war; and *PZ88 Madeline*, commandeered in 1940 when Mr Willis was the owner and Herbert Everson the skipper, was attached to Dover.[51] *PZ107 Renovelle* was a Mousehole boat operated by the Madron family; she was released to resume fishing before the end of the war, as was the *PZ123 Mayon Castle*.[52] Pre-war skippers were Edward Harvey Richards & Dick Hall; in 1948 the crew included William Balls (Lowestoft), John Nichols and WH Tonkin.[53]

Above left: *PZ18 United Boys* outside the Old Harbour, Newlyn. Source, Raymond Tonkin
Above right: John Foster Tonkin (Sn) wearing insignia of HMS Drake. Source, J F Tonkin

The following account about the experience of one of the requisitioned fishing boats, *United Boys*, is based on family papers and stories that John Foster Tonkin Sn told his son: [54]

One day there appeared at Newlyn a number of naval personnel from Plymouth who walked up and down the quay several times and then made their selection of boats to commandeer into the Royal Naval Service. *PZ18 United Boys* was one of the six motor fishing vessels (MFVs) allocated to serve on the Western side of the United Kingdom, in the Bristol Channel, the Irish Sea and the Firth of Clyde.[55] The crews of these vessels were offered the opportunity to serve as members of the Royal Navy and operate under naval command on their own boats or the alternative was 'coming ashore, leaving their boat to others' and being conscripted into the armed forces.

The boat was collectively owned and crewed by two sets of brothers, who were also cousins, each having one quarter share. All four men, William and Peter Simons, and William Henry and John Foster Tonkin, chose the Royal Navy, rather than abandon their boat to others. They served under HMS Drake, a Plymouth 'shore' establishment (the name was shown on both their hats and uniform); two became petty officer engineer and chief petty officer and the other two able seamen.

PZ18 United Boys was built on the quayside, below the ferry steps at East Looe, Cornwall in 1934 and launched into the river at a high autumn tide, a 49ft lugger - 14.6ft beam and 6ft draft, 23.18 tons, on oak frame with pine decking and planking. The arrival in Newlyn of a 'new fishing boat built to the order of Mr William Henry Tonkin' (the father of the brothers William Henry and John Foster) was recorded in the Cornishman.[56]

Along with the other five boats commandeered at this time, *PZ18 United Boys* was sent to the shipyard at Falmouth to be converted and painted grey for War service. Although it was fitted out with guns and other equipment, the men received no training.[57] Other boats were fitted with machine guns and carried soldiers at first although later the crew had to work the machine guns.[58] John Foster Tonkin Sn never talked about the boat being armed with any mounted gun, but he did say that there was a naval cutlass on board, presumably to repel anyone wishing to come on board uninvited.

---

[51] Perry 2001:71.
[52] McWilliams 2007:87
[53] Stevenson Exhibition, April 3 2010
[54] Tonkin NA 2249
[55] The United Boys was also listed as a minesweeping drifter at Dartmouth under Plymouth Command in 1942 <www.naval-history. net>
[56] 50 Years Ago, *Cornishman* October 11 1984
[57] Raymond Tonkin, in conversation
[58] Perry 2001:40

PZ18 United Boys' first posting was to the port of Padstow on the north Cornish coast where the crew undertook depth-charge duties. This may have been a euphemism for something more secretive. JFT Sn wrote, 'our job was patrolling the coast and we sank one mine at Tintagel and the next day another was washed up at Harline Bay and three of us with a Lieutenant rolled it about 250 feet across the beach and secured it to a tree on the edge of the cliff with the Police keeping everyone at a safe distance. That afternoon naval personnel from Plymouth came and made it safe'.

He said that 'people' were sometimes on board when they went to sea; and they and the crew often dropped depth charges, which were timed with a stopwatch to record the depth when they detonated. He wrote 'a month or two later - before going to Scotland - we had a depth charge trial and were almost blown up by our own depth charge; as it was faulty in its parts'.

Until the release of government documents in 2006, historians were unaware of the U-boat death trap off the Cornish coast. A U-boat commander had discovered a gap in the minefield between Cornwall and Ireland that allowed supply ships in to Cardiff and Bristol. Details of three sunken German submarines lying just seven miles off Newquay were reported to the 26th Annual Shipwrecks, Diving and Marine Archaeology Conference Plymouth[59].

Just what was the *United Boys* doing off Padstow during this period of Naval operations? Who were those 'people' who were on board? Was she dropping depth charges on enemy submarines without the crew knowing what was going on?

After Padstow, the *United Boys* was sent to Lamlash on the Isle of Arran in the Firth of Clyde.[60] Lamlash was a naval base during both world wars, the ships taking advantage of the shelter afforded by the bay and nearby Holy Island. All six of the Newlyn fishing boats serving in the Western Approaches were at some time operating in the firth of Clyde out of Lamlash.

From Lamlash, the *United Boys* went to Northern Ireland, where it was stationed from November 1942 to June 1944, operating out of Belfast and Bangor. At least two other Newlyn motor fishing vessels were there, *the Cornishman* (as a Kite Balloon Tender) and the *Peel Castle*.

On one occasion, at Bangor, the crew of the *United Boys* was apprehended for smuggling cigarettes and tobacco, which they had got from the Americans. At the Navy hearing, the officer said that it was the first time he had met a bunch of Cornish Pirates![61]

Below: John Foster Tonkin (b1907) holding a cup of tea with others at Barry Docks, South Wales where *United Boys* was stationed in June 1944 for another twelve months. Source, JF Tonkin

---

[59] Western Morning News, February 11 2008
[60] The United Boys was listed as being a minesweeping drifter at Lamlash in 1942. See <www.naval-history.net>
[61] Raymond Tonkin, in conversation

Defences

While the requisitioned Newlyn boats and their crews helped defend the western coast, other precautions were taken nearer home. Defences were set up. Land was requisitioned to erect two pillboxes under the War Emergency Act, 1939. These were small concrete forts given their name because of their shape.[62] One was erected at Sandy Cove on the south side of Newlyn while the other was at Tolcarne. There was an army Barracks on top of J H Bennetts Coal store (later Stevenson's fish store).

Air raid shelters were erected, one in front of the Newlyn Mission,[63] or buildings were converted for the purpose, including the five large fish tanks at the Stevenson's Trewarveneth store, which were encased in concrete to become air raid shelter No 47. Cecil Jenkin's father and his neighbour Ted Collins built one under the loft in their yard in the Coombe.

The Coombe River was dammed at the main road bridge to provide water for firefighting. Firefighting was an important precaution due to the threat of incendiary bombs and a fire station was set up in the fish stores by Newlyn Bridge manned by the Auxiliary Fire Service under Mr Leslie White, acting head teacher at Tolcarne School.

Left: Sid and Bert Perrott sit with Mary and Amy Hichens on Newlyn Green Beach with the barbed wire fence of wartime clearly visible behind. From Louise Hancock

Some beaches were mined and had anti-tank devices installed, like those between Long Rock and Marazion. Seymour Cooke who joined the Duke of Cornwall's Light Infantry and helped construct the beach defences, claimed that the longest run of barbed wire was from Newlyn Harbour to Marazion.[64] Although some beaches were cordoned off with barbed wire, access was allowed. Roberta St Claire remembers her auntie Aggie taking her in the pushchair to the beach near Whitby where a soldier from the TA raised a curl of barbed wire to let them through so they could fill the pushchair with driftwood for the fire.[65] Similarly, between Newlyn and Larrigan, families were allowed on to the beach.[66]

Air raids, bombs and shelters

It seems that Newlyn did not take the threat of bombing seriously at first, so that when it happened it came as a surprise. The events described below (which sound remarkably similar) must have provided clear warnings of the coming danger:

> Without warning, flying low along the beach came two German aeroplanes... Everyone was terrified and running in different directions... My friends and I were in the sea and in fear we dived under the water, holding our breath for as long as we could. When we surfaced, we could see the planes turn out over the sea and come back again over the beach. Just about then two motor torpedo boats that were docked at Newlyn came to our rescue... as suddenly as the aeroplanes appeared, they vanished over the skyline.[67]

> Newlyn beach was crowded with mothers and children happily sailing their boats or shrimping in the pools, when three German aircraft came in over the sea very fast and so low that the pilots could be seen. Fortunately, they made no attack there but went on to St Ives where they bombed the gasworks after machine-gunning a bus on the way. On another occasion, incendiaries dropped on the rocks at Tolcarne, and on a house near the South Pier, failed to ignite.[68]

Geoffrey Garnier, who was the officer in charge of the Newlyn Home Guard in the early part of the war, recorded that bombs were first dropped in the Newlyn area on November 7 1940:

[62] <www.pillbox-study-group.org.uk>
[63] Jenkin 2009:170-188
[64] V Acton & D Carter *Operation Cornwall, 1940-1944* (Landfall publications, 1994)
[65] Roberta St Claire, *Evacuee Aged Two*, NA 1793
[66] Jenkin 2009:170-188
[67] Clitheroe 1990:30
[68] Jenkin 2009:173

Planes approached from the West. The first stick was released over Sheffield, skated over the hill and fell in the sea just beyond the North Pier of the Harbour. The second stick fell in fields above the village and did no harm. The remainder of the attack was concentrated on Penzance and out of the Platoon area.[69]

Was this the first raid on Newlyn, which according to Ricky Clitheroe[70] happened on a Sunday evening in 1940? When the siren sounded, he had taken refuge with his 'uncle' and 'aunt' Charlie and Liz Tresize, in the old adit that led from the road to Jacob's well in the garden of Well Cottage (now called Magnolia Cottage). The entrance to the tunnel is the plain plywood door in the side of the garden wall on St Peter's Hill; it is still there today.[71] As now, the tunnel (which is carved out of the granite) was padlocked, but the Tresizes had the key. It must have been very uncomfortable and eerie in the dark and dampness with the sound of water from the well at the end of the tunnel, but it was fortunate that the family took refuge there rather than in the kitchen shed in their small orchard behind the cottage, as that night the shed received a direct hit and all the glass in the windows was blasted out of the cottage.

Garnier records another bomb attack on May 27 1941 when enemy planes attacked Newlyn Harbour, dropping several bombs during which the buildings adjoining the Harbour were heavily sprayed with machine gun and cannon fire. This occasion saw one of the few fatalities in Newlyn. According to Garnier:

> [The] enemy planes attacked Newlyn Harbour, dropping several bombs and making a series of runs during which the buildings adjoining the Harbour were heavily sprayed with MG[72] and cannon fire. The Platoon was in possession of twelve Lewis MGs on loan from the RNO. These were quickly in position and fire was opened on the enemy planes. During one run Volunteer Basil Chiffers, who was acting as loader to Sergeant Stevenson, was hit and killed by a cannon shell. There was a second casualty (unknown) who was hit in the ear by a MG bullet. [73]

Sergeant Stevenson was also injured in this raid. Most probably it was the same raid that forced Charles Symons' father to lie on the step of Newlyn Post Office when a German plane came down the Coombe, machine-gunning as it passed through Newlyn heading for the harbour.[74]

The other event that is remembered on the day that Chiffers died was the attack on the coal hulk *Cretehill*. This was a very large ferro-concrete barge that had been there since 1925 and was used for the storage of coal for the fishing fleet. According to Billy Stevenson, her original iron deckhouse had decayed and a galvanised iron shed had been erected on her deck together with a crane. As the hulk already rested

on the bottom of the harbour, there was no dramatic sinking, and there was much amusement when the traitor William Joyce, known as Lord Haw Haw who broadcast propaganda bulletins claimed that an aircraft carrier had been sunk.[75]

Right: The hulk *Cretehill* before WW2. Photo by George Curnow. Source, George Hoare

Adrian Nicholas remembers swimming with his sister into the side of the bombed hulk, *Cretehill* before it was broken up and towed away on March 15 1949. His first memory of the war was hearing a bomb fall when he was being pushed up Kneebone's Lane in his pram. Another family story was of his sister walking back to Newlyn along New Road when four bombs were dropped near the Western Green.[76]

[69] Geoffrey Garnier, Historical Notes on Newlyn/Mousehole Platoon, Unpublished paper NA164
[70] Clitheroe 1990:34-36
[71] Newlyn's Water, Newlyn Environment Group 2007:13
[72] Machine Gun
[73] Garnier NA164
[74] Charles Symons, in conversation
[75] Barnes NA2140; Jenkin 2009:174; Perry 2001:58
[76] Adrian Nicholas, in conversation.

Unfortunately, Garnier's account comes to an end in July 1941, upon his retirement from the Home Guard, so that it is difficult to establish accurately where and when bombs fell. The newspapers were not allowed to name places in their reports, so we must rely on oral accounts. Liz Harman remembers a bomb falling on the playing field near Trewarveneth Farm in the early days of the war before there were Morrison shelters (the table ones made of steel or iron). It was in the evening; they heard a whine, and her mother grabbed her and her friend and pushed them under the dining table. There was more than one bomb that night, but Liz doesn't remember where the others fell.[77]

George Barnes, Cecil Jenkin and Billy Stevenson all report seeing bombs fall on the Larrigan rocks. It was Cecil Jenkin's first experience of bombs. He was playing in a barn at Zimmerman Cot in the Coombe with the farmer's elder son, Glynn Ellery.

> We heard a low-flying aircraft. Glynn said, 'It's a German', and I took off for home, running in the same direction as the plane... As I pounded down the farm road, I saw the bomb doors open and four bombs drop out. They landed on the Larrigan rocks... Presumably, the intended target was the Western National bus garage at Wherrytown, which had a large factory-like roof.[78]

George Barnes remembers being in his garden and hearing an aircraft:

> Looking up I saw this bomber come from behind the trees at about 300 feet, as I watched I saw a stick of bombs fall away from it, they screamed over my head and exploded on the Larrigan Rocks just 400 yards away.

On this occasion, the bombs dropped harmlessly in the sea.

Lane Reddin Terrace was badly damaged by bombs that landed in the back gardens, breaking all the windows. According to George Hoare, just a toddler when the bombs fell, it was a night-time raid and the force of the bomb (dropped up at Andrawednack) dislodged a large block of granite, which fell through the roof of Cressars (George's home) demolishing the bed from which he had been snatched when the siren sounded just a short time before. His grandmother's house Homealong was also strafed by bullets from the lone German fighter aircraft.[79]

Both Cecil Jenkin[80] and Billy Stevenson[81] record unexploded bombs out-the-Green in January 1941 which caused children to stay away from school. Billy was at school in Hayle with Godfrey and Sydney Stevens whose grandfather was Peter Hosking, the sailmaker who lived at Green Rocks. One morning the boys could not go home because there were two unexploded bombs near their house. One of the bombs was in the Gendalls' yard at Primrose Terrace and one next-door in Granny Barnes' kitchen. Philip Gendall (who worked at the quarry), his wife Bessie (née Barnes) and her mother Granny Barnes were evacuated to their daughter Grace Bassett's home, Rose Villa on St Peter's Hill. Grace recalls the bomb ticking away in her Granny's kitchen while she helped retrieve things from her mother's kitchen. The bomb had to be left for 100 hours after the bomb disposal unit from Plymouth had done their work. The unit consisted of 'fifteen beautiful young ensign men' who slept in the beds in Mrs Gendall's four bedrooms 'with boots an' all'. The cottage was badly damaged inside and there was mud everywhere but the roof was almost intact. When it was all over, Philip Gendall persuaded his daughter to treat the men to a drink at the Fishermen's Arms, where they all shook hands. According to Billy Stevenson, after the bombs were made safe, one was given to Mr Plumbridge, the publican at the Fisherman's Arms.

The Gendalls had two near misses during the war. The second was when one of the gas-filled barrage balloons, that were used to protect the stone boats when they came into Newlyn Harbour to load stone at the South Pier, burst and landed on Mrs Gendall's roof. The cottage caught fire. The fire brigade arrived in time to put out the fire but there was water all over the kitchen. As it was a Saturday, Bessie Gendall had gone shopping in Penzance with another daughter, so Grace was called again to help her dad as the windows were broken, the roof was damaged, and the water was racing down the staircase and into the kitchen.[82]

---

[77] Liz Harman, in conversation.

[78] Jenkin 2009:173

[79] George Hoare, in conversation

[80] Jenkin 2009:72

[81] Perry 2001:62

[82] Handwritten transcript of an interview with Mrs Bassett. Papers from Golowan Local Audio Archive belonging to Pat Waller. PLHG Archive, Morrab Library.

This branch of the Home Guard met at Penzance. Jack Williams, middle row, far right lived in Kenstella Road during the war. He used to guard at the Battery Rocks. Source, Linda Holmes

The Home Guard

The archive is lucky to contain a number of original documents that belonged to Geoffrey Garnier, who was asked by Capt C E Venning to organise and form the Newlyn/Mousehole Section of the Local Defence Volunteers (LDV) on May 23 1940. The documents include a paper entitled *Historical Notes on Newlyn/Mousehole Platoon* by Geoffrey Garnier (NA164), an old map marked *Secret* and titled *Group Signals HG* (NA169) and a WW2 notebook of secret WW2 codes (NA 224). The documents, which were donated to the archive by Pat Garnier, also contain newspaper cuttings and photos of Geoffrey and his wife Jill. Bob Harrison has examined these documents and fitted Geoffrey's story into wider research he has been doing about the Home Guard.

Jill and Geoffrey Garnier during WW2.
Source, Pat Garnier

Garnier's appointment followed Anthony Eden's broadcast on the BBC's Home Service on May 14 1940, in which he urged men to join the newly formed Local Defence Volunteers (LDV) by registering at their local police stations. Within 24 hours, 250,000 men had registered nationally.[83]

What happened next is best reported in the words of Geoffrey Garnier, the new section leader:
On the 27th May, Volunteers were enrolled at the British Legion Hall, Newlyn. I appointed Mr. R Hosken (sic) to be my Assistant. On 28th May, Volunteers from the Mousehole area were enrolled in

---

[83] Bob Harrison, *Notes on the Home Guard* NA2262

the Legion Hall, Mousehole, Mr E P Waters being appointed as Sub/Section Leader. Within a month, the strength of the Section had reached 248. [84]

Garnier, the son of two artist parents, was himself an engraver and lived at Orchard Cottage in Newlyn (telephone number *Penzance 197).* His deputy, Richard (Dick) Hosking was a WW1 Veteran and local builder who had the telephone number *Penzance 809.* The section that they led was responsible for an area bounded on the west by Lamorna River up to Drift; on the north by the Lands End Road from Drift to Four Lanes End; on the east by Newlyn River from Four Lanes End to the sea. The platoon had seven posts to man at Higher Kemyel; Castallack - Kemyel Road; New Reservoir; Tresvennack; Symonds Farm, Tresvennack; Paul Church Tower and Mousehole Pier. They also had a Road Block at Chywoone Corner.

The local defence volunteers did not last long, and at the suggestion of Winston Churchill, became the Home Guard on August 23 1940. Many who had come forward originally were veterans of older conflicts; some of these were thanked and politely turned down.[85] Despite this, the LDV was nicknamed 'Look-Duck-Vanish';[86] changing its name did not alter its image and the new Home Guard became 'Dad's Army'.

Initially, meetings were held in the Liberal Club above Stevenson's Pilchard Store. Later, they moved to the old Drill Hall, above Penzer House. Before the war this had been occupied by Primrose Dairy but was vacant when the Home Guard took it over. Later it became a button factory. Geoffrey Garnier has left a description of his policy in managing a number of incidents:

On the 7th Sept 1940, the following message was received: 'State of Alarm. All Posts will be manned and stay so until recalled. Enemy agents are expected to land by parachute. Gas attack with smoke expected at dawn to cover stronger attack.' The Platoon went to action stations and remained on duty until 1030 hrs the following morning.

During the night of the same day - 8th Sept - a state of Alert was ordered and all Posts were manned.

On 22nd Sept 1941, a State of Alarm was in operation all day. A message was received: 'Invasion expected at 1530 hrs.' In the evening, a warning was received that enemy parachutists were expected to land at dawn.

On each of these Alarms, the method, which I adopted, for turning out the men was by driving through the area accompanied by a bugler. On the first occasion - 7th Sept - on making my first round of the Posts I was informed by the men that each had been visited by a Special Constable who was outraged at the whole proceeding; stated that I was suffering from an attack of hysterics; that the men had no right to be under arms; and ordered them all home to bed!! Accompanied by an armed party I went in search of the supposed Fifth columnist. He (and perhaps myself) was fortunate in failing to make contact. [87]

Warwick Trahair, Garfield Kneebone and Johnny Blewett. W Stevenson's bread van (in the background) was used as an ambulance. Source, Billy Stevenson Collection

In June and July 1940, the records show that a very mixed assortment of weapons was taken on charge and there was also ammunition.[88] According to Billy Stevenson, the men were armed with old Springfield rifles from the United States. These had arrived in boxes, thickly coated with yellow grease. The men were given a rifle each and they had to remove the grease with rags and paraffin before they could be used. By June 1941, the platoon had a number of Lewis machine guns; Stevenson records that 15-20 Lewis machine guns were held in the armoury at Newlyn until 1943.

---

[84] Geoffrey Garnier, *Historical Notes on Newlyn/Mousehole Platoon,* Unpublished paper NA164
[85] Jenkin, 2009:170
[86] Harrison NA2262
[87] Garnier NA164
[88] Harrison NA2262

Because his father and his uncle were in the Home Guard, the young Billy Stevenson would go up to the Drill Hall several nights a week to watch them practising with rifles as there was a firing range inside surrounded by sandbags. When the men were on manoeuvres, Billy and his friends Bobby Swanson and Lewis Brown (all in the Sea Scouts) would sometimes act as messengers as they had bikes.

Machine gun practice took place at Balswidden, a disused clay pit. For this, the men borrowed the machine guns used to protect the boats in the harbour, returning them by 5am next morning. When the Home Guard was issued with a Browning light machine gun, Burt Dyer from Mousehole altered it so that it fired 20 instead of 10 automatic shots. He was a precision engineer who did maintenance work on the Belgian and French boats as well as being a sergeant in the Home Guard. [89]

In April 1941 reference is made to the battalion reserve of ammunition being stored at Trengwainton, Penzance and consisting of four cases of cartons (1,500 x 4), seven cases of bandoliers (1,200 x 7) and a case of twelve bandoliers plus loose thirty-five rounds totalling 15,155. In the same month the following equipment and clothing was taken on charge: 409 jackets, 410 trousers, 416 caps (350 in one sack), 226 brassards, 100 field dressings, six rifle slings, six pull-thro's, six oil bottles and assorted quantities of buckles, buttons and rings. [90]

A number of vehicles were requisitioned for use by the Home Guard. They included the Stevenson lorry FAF 25, W S Stevenson's Renault (PCV 62), a Royal Enfield motorbike purchased specifically for the use of the dispatch rider, and Dick Hosking's lorry. When on manoeuvres the Stevenson van, driven by Basil Stevenson and used for the bread round during the day, became the ambulance and Basil a stretcher-bearer. Basil Stevenson's Home Guard stretcher-bearer certificate, dated November 28 1941 and signed C E Venning, can be seen in Billy Stevenson's archive.

Right: Bakers van with 'W Stevenson & Sons High Class Bakers & Confectioners Newlyn' on it, c1936/7. Outside garage in Trewarveneth St. House behind is where Liz Harman lived. Source, Billy Stevenson Collection

---

Night Operation, 4.00 a.m. 30th July 1940

The alarm will come into operation at 4 a.m. Posts should be manned as soon afterwards as possible. The road block at Jarvis's Gateway will be manned by men from the Reservoir Post as arranged. Two unarmed men will be sent to each petrol station in our area. (Mousehole section leader please note). If possible they will carry a heavy hammer. In the event of a real show they would smash the pumps.

Gas masks and identity cards MUST be carried. Live ammunition will be carried, but no rifle is to be loaded.

Mr.B.Stevenson will act as despatch rider between myself and Capt. Vennings house. When recognised he should be passed through at once.

In addition to the road block at the top of Paul Hill, Castallack will hold the Lamorna-Castallack Junction (Three corner pool).

At both road blocks there will be a man with a red lamp. He stands ALONE. 20 yards behind him will be an armed man. All others on the block will be out of sight. UNDER NO CIRCUMSTANCES MUST THEY REVEAL THEIR PRESENCE UNLESS ORDERED TO DO SO. All cars will be stopped wether they give the recoginition signal or not.

The recoginition signal given by troops or L.D.V. will be 'Two light flashes - or two sounds on the horn. Then a pause, then repeat.' To pass on they must show their identity cards or AB640.

All messages must be prefixed by the words 'Practise repeat - practise repeat - practise' written thus.

Umpires will wear a white singlet on each arm.

A log of all messages received or sent must be kept and handed to me at 6.00 a.m. when the operation ends.

At 6.00 a.m. all men will disperse.

Geoffrey S Garnier.

At the end of July 1941 owing to ill health, Geoffrey Garnier resigned command of the Platoon, and 2nd Lieutenant Richard Hosking was appointed to take his place. Garnier left a list of the Platoon's achievements up to that time:

> The Platoon had the honour to be selected by Colonel Watson-Smyth to carry out various demonstrations before a number of Regular and HG Officers. Of these, the most outstanding was a demonstration attack in arrowhead

[89] Perry, 2001:53-57
[90] Harrison NA2262

formation on Trivida Moor. For the first time in the Zone what was later known as Battle Innoculation was employed. A large quantity of explosive charges was laid on the Moor and was fired electrically as each round of the attack was made. In this way, a very realistic effect of shell and mortar fire was obtained, the mines actually exploding amongst the men as they crossed open ground. There were no casualties, and at the end of the demonstration, Lord Fortescue congratulated the Platoon very highly on the way in which the Exercise had been carried out.[91]

Eighteen months after Garnier left the platoon, a national reorganisation of the Home Guard took place and Cornwall was divided into North and West Sectors. Newlyn became one of five battalions in the West Cornwall Sector. The 12th Battalion or Lands End Battalion was formed on December 1 1942 and had its HQ

at Penzance. It was affiliated to the Duke of Cornwall's Light Infantry (DCLI). The Commanding Officer was Lt Col the Lord St Levan. The Land's End Battalion had six platoons including the Newlyn Platoon, consisting of Paul, Newlyn and Mousehole.[92]

Left: William Sampson Stevenson (top row, second from left) was the Controlling Officer for Fish Allocation in Newlyn during the war years. Taken outside Stevenson's Island Stores in 1940. Also in the picture are Charlie Mitchell (extreme right) and Frank Hosking (seated, in overalls). The rest are Lowestoft merchants. Source, Billy Stevenson Collection

William Sampson Stevenson had been one of the first to join the Local Defence Volunteers, and after the reorganisation, he became a 1st Lieutenant, working in signals at Trereife in the Coombe, the home of the Le Grice family. He had to be at the fish market by eight each morning, allocating fish. The Newlyn Allocation Committee covered coastal areas extending from Long Rock to Sennen Cove. Under Emergency Powers (Defence) Orders, the government controlled both the allocation of fish and the price at which it was sold. At midday, William Sampson would go home to dinner and then return to work in the afternoon. Often from there he would go directly to Trereife (where he had a bunk) and could be on Home Guard duty all night, going straight back to the market next morning.[93]

Away at War

At the start of the war, a steady stream of young people, and older men who had served in WW1, signed up for the armed forces. Charlie Shears (picture on the right, source June Shears) was in the Royal Navy in WW1. In WW2, he joined the Merchant Navy and worked on the Russian convoys, on the *Empire Tide*.

Ronald Shears (Charlie's son) with Jacky Everson and 'Boy' Chiffers went together to sign up but only the first two were accepted. They served on the *Prince of Wales*, which was blown up, but they survived by jumping from the sinking ship, holding hands.[94] The seventeen-year-old Basil Chiffers joined the Home Guard but became a casualty of war, shot by an enemy aircraft.

Lt R Davies was in charge of a bomb disposal section when an unexploded 2,240lb bomb dropped near to St Paul's Cathedral in September 1940. Born in Newlyn, his family emigrated to Canada, but he returned to take part in both the world wars. The bomb near St Pauls was buried 28 feet in the ground and two lorries in tandem were needed to haul it out.

[91] Garnier NA164
[92] Harrison NA2262
[93] Perry 2001:53-57
[94] Alan Shears, in conversation

It was placed on a lorry and driven to Hackney Marshes by Lt Davies where it was exploded, causing a 100ft crater.[95]

Harvey Richards (picture on the right, source Ruth Richards) joined the Royal Naval Volunteer Reserve in 1940, serving on board *HMML 282* of the 2nd Motor Launch Flotilla. In December 1943, he made an unexpected visit to his family at Tolcarne. This was his story:

> In 1943, *ML (Motor Launch) 282* was at Plymouth and we were directed to sail to Milford Haven to escort a number of American Landing Craft bound for Normandy. We had rounded the Lizard on our course for Land's End when a South Westerly gale blew up and I persuaded the skipper to seek shelter in Newlyn. While he reported to Admiral Pilcher, I took the opportunity to call in at my home, 12 New Road, looking forward to a pasty perhaps! It seemed that in no time, the Skipper was knocking at the front door to say that Plymouth had ordered us to sea forthwith as the Americans had already left Milford Haven without an escort. [96]

That night the weather was very rough but when *ML 282* came to Wolf Rock the sea was perfectly flat and ink black. A U-boat also looking for the convoy had grounded on the rocks, splitting its oil tanks!

Edward 'Sam' Munkley (picture on left, source, Adrian Nicholas) served in the 8th Army; he went to North Africa, Italy and Monte Cassino. He had a piece of shrapnel in his leg, which was never removed so that he had a limp. After the war, he drove an excavator at the quarry. He was an honoured guest at the Gaiety cinema and his family went free when the film Dunkirk was shown.[97]

Many men were mentioned in despatches for distinguished service and received medals, like Gunner George W H Hoare who served in the Royal Artillery (certificate on right, source George Hoare). When he returned home after the war, he put his medals in a cupboard and forbade his family to touch them. Such was the horror that was recorded in the acts of bravery that the medals represented.

By the KING'S Order the name of *Gunner W. H. Hoare*, *Royal Artillery*, was published in the London Gazette on *9th August, 1945* as mentioned in a Despatch for distinguished service. I am charged to record His Majesty's high appreciation.

Secretary of State for War

Another hero of WW1 was Newlyner, Richard James Nicholas. He was summoned to Chyandour Barracks during WW2 and asked to be the coastguard at Lamorna. He readily accepted an army uniform, a Lee Enfield 303 rifle, and taking his son Adrian (aged 6), they were away.

Adrian remembers sleeping in a green wooden hut outside the row of cottages in Lamorna Cove. Just him and his father.[98]

Far left: Nicholas Peake won the Distinguished Service Medal in 1944. Source, Glenys Peake

Left: Leading Wren Joyce Richards from New Road Newlyn. Source, Ruth Richards

This is a small selection of Newlyners who served in WW2 and readers are urged to provide information of others to record in the archive.

[95] Unknown Newspaper report NA1857
[96] Harvey Richards, digital recording, *Newlyn at War*
[97] Adrian Nicholas NA 1958
[98] Adrian Nicholas NA 1136

Belgian Refugees

...a little port from which a fleet of 40 Belgian motor trawlers with 300 men ply their trade and support a large and flourishing colony. Women with bright handkerchiefs around their heads hang washing unselfconsciously from front windows and dry haddock (sic) in the sun. You meet youngsters chattering French or carrying on games with little English friends in the lingua franca of childhood. The behaviour of all the refugees has been admirable.

Daily Telegraph August 18 1940

During the war, most of Newlyn's bigger boats were called up for Royal Navy service as auxiliaries and their place was taken by a large fleet of Belgian trawlers. The Belgian fleet was Britain's most important allied fishing fleet during the war, with 226 trawlers,[99] representing ninety-five percent of the Belgian fishing fleet. It was dispersed in the fishing villages of Newlyn, Brixham, Fleetwood and Milford Haven. The small boats or shrimp catchers went to Brixham, the middleclass trawlers to Newlyn and the deep-sea trawlers were sent to Fleetwood or to Milford Haven. Some of the Belgian boats were ex-British sailing smacks, which had been converted to motor trawlers in the 1920s,[100] such as *0152 Oceans' Gift* and *N63 Sincerity*. Some of the Belgian boats came directly to Newlyn in 1940, while others came from Brixham in 1943 at a time when work at that port became focused on preparations for the Normandy landings.[101]

The departure of the fishing boats from Belgium carrying refugees as well as fishermen's families was a horrendous affair. Marie Vantorre aged fourteen remembers helping her mother pack small bundles of essentials for her four siblings, the youngest only eighteen months, while her father and the crew took provisions to the harbour by horse and cart. The young Norbert Bil, who crossed with his father Camile Bil and his grandfather Franz Bil (both fishermen), recalls several accompanying craft being sunk by German aircraft with all on board lost when they crossed in May 1940. Jozef Couwyzer, a little nine-year-old refugee from Heist, made the hazardous journey in his father's boat *Z10 Marie Joseph*. The Couwyzer family had not wanted to leave Belgium but like other boat owners, they believed that the German army would requisition their boat, so it was a choice between leaving their home and saving the boat or keeping the house and losing the ship. They chose to come. Unfortunately, *Z10 Marie Joseph* was laid up for its yearly overhaul and the crew had a bare twenty-four hours to make it seaworthy. It was too little time so that when they left Belgium to join the forty or so fishing boats from Heist and Zeebrugge at Dunkirk, it was not really ready and would not have reached England if *Z9 Minerva*, owned by Jozef's uncle Medard Duysers (who later lived at Mousehole), had not towed it to England.

The Goutsmit family were aboard the last boat to leave Ostend as the Germans were entering the town. As they passed Dunkirk, the town was burning, and the evacuation was in full swing. They came to Newlyn but could not enter, as the harbour was already full of Belgian trawlers; they were moved on to Milford Haven and were there for two years before coming back to Newlyn.

The Vantorre's boat went to Dunkirk in company with about forty others, some of which were sunk on the way, but because of bombing their stay was brief and they went on to Dieppe. There was no relief there either and for several nights in company with hundreds of others, the family sheltered in deep caves, leaving only the skippers in the boats. When the situation worsened all fishing boats were ordered to sail for Britain, and Marie Vantorre vividly remembers sailing out of Dieppe with a cooking pot on her head as a crude protection against bombs and bullets.

Jozef Couwyzer recalls being anchored close to the beach at Dunkirk, under constant attack from the German Stukas. The boats were not allowed to pick up British soldiers who might have been deserters, although paradoxically when the ships got back to England about forty-eight Belgian trawlers mainly from Heist and Zeebrugge went back to evacuate 4800 British soldiers, many of the boats making several journeys.

---

[99] R Vanhove, *Vlaamse Vissers in Groot-Brittannie* NA 1681,1682

[100] Raymond Peake NA 1683

[101] Much of this section is based on accounts compiled by Cecil Jenkin in 1990 and Margaret Perry in 2004. Both have personal recollections of the Belgians during WW2. Cecil Jenkin wrote to the mayors of Ostend and Zeebrugge asking for information, his letters were published in the local press, and he received a number of replies telling the story of the Belgian experience. This is reproduced in his book: Cecil Jenkin, *Newlyn: A View from Street-an-Nowan*, Bodmin 2009:177-184. Margaret Perry compiled a collection of material based on correspondence with the Belgian, Jozef Couwyzer, who spent part of his childhood as a refugee in Newlyn and has donated this to the archive. Billy Stevenson's autobiography, edited by Margaret Perry and fully referenced earlier, is another important source of information in this chapter

The experience of arrival in Britain was unpleasant and traumatic for most of the refugees. The boat crew and their families were often interred on the boat for several days, although the coastguards and other services provided necessary supplies daily. Then everyone was taken ashore for medical examinations and interrogation. All new arrivals had to be registered and each received an identity card; they also had to undergo a vetting process to establish that they were not spies. Often the families were split up; Jozef C at the age of nine was separated from his parents for thirteen months before being reunited first at Penzance, and then coming to live at Newlyn in the previously condemned cottage at 6 Farmer's Meadow.

The Belgian Fleet

Belgian and French refugee ships just after the fall of France, 1941. Source, Billy Stevenson Collection

Sheila Thomas was ten years old when the Belgian refugees arrived on their fishing boats just as the quarry blasted off, the women dressed all in black. She remembers the men picking winkles off the rocks at the mouth of the Tolcarne stream, which Sheila and the other the children were not allowed to eat.[102] Another strange custom was that of drying small megrim on the washing lines outside their homes. When the men could not fish because of bad weather, the megrim were strung up in the engine rooms of their boats.[103] Many of the Belgians became local characters, and they were given Newlyn nicknames, so the skipper of *0246 Frans Elsa* was nicknamed *the Rat* and her owner *the Burgomaster*.[104]

Despite some bad feeling, the Belgian fleet and community gave a boost to Newlyn's economy. The harbour had its small inshore fleet of Cornish pilchard drivers but the Belgian trawlers landed the bulk of the fish and made money for the fish market. The Belgians rented premises like the lofts in the Island Store in the Fradgan, which were used to store their nets. Local businesses benefitted from the Belgians. But the Belgian fishermen paid a high price for their fish. In the early part of the war, the Belgian trawlers carried an armed soldier; the soldiers wore distinctive shoulder flashes, containing a rifle and an anchor.[105] Later, if German aircraft attacked a fishing boat, the Admiralty suggested that fishermen could fight back with a gun that fired grenades, or a rocket that fired a parachute. Fishing boats with machine guns were advised to stay together as the fire from several craft was a more effective deterrent than the fire from a single gun.[106] Eventually, the trawlers were fitted with Lewis guns and machine guns, but this did not help the *Charles*

---

[102] Sheila Thomas, in conversation
[103] Raymond Peake, Archive Day June 28 2010
[104] McWilliams NA1419
[105] Cecil Jenkin, in conversation
[106] The Second World War <HistoryShelf.org> September 23 2010

Madeleine. This was a brand new boat; George Peake & Sons made the trawl doors. It left Newlyn to fish in July 1940 and it was never seen again except for its punt, which was washed up on the beach full of bullet holes.[107] In October, the fishing fleet was attacked by E-boats and the *Marguerite Simone* was sunk off Lamorna Cove. In all, twenty-four Belgian trawlers and fifty-nine lives were lost off the western shores.

The importance of the Belgian contribution to the war effort was recognised when King George VI and Queen Elizabeth visited Newlyn North Pier in August 1942. Two of the men in the photograph on the right are Camiel Bil and his father Frans Bil. Sources, Douglas Williams (left) and Billy Stevenson (right)

Not all the Belgian trawlers went fishing as some were commandeered by the Admiralty, including *H11 Jan Virginie*, brought over by Petrus Dewaele and *H41 Frank*, owned by George de Summers. According to Billy Stevenson, about half the Belgian boats at Newlyn were at some time requisitioned in this way such as *H28 De Hoop*, which had carried its owner Jeroom Dhoore with his wife Stephanie and their children Jozef and Simone from Belgium, and fished out of Mousehole before it was requisitioned. The *Suzanne Adrienne* was used by the Navy as an escort boat at Newlyn; its skipper (from Grimsby) made a trawl net and caught fish that was sold to raise funds for the officers' mess housed in the Newlyn Mission and a WREN brought them to the fish market each day on a barrow.[108] The owners of the requisitioned boats were given £4 weekly as compensation for not being able to fish and they and the crew had to find work in order to survive. The boats were used as escort boats, or for mine watching, which involved watching at night to see where enemy parachutes dropped mines. Unfortunately, some of the boats commandeered by the Navy were eventually returned in very poor condition. When *H69 Maris Stella* was returned to the Rappe family it was unseaworthy, and while being towed from Dartmouth it ran onto rocks and was a total loss.

Fortunately, there was no shortage of work on the fishing boats. Georges de Summers bought *PZ459 Boy Don* and fitted her for trawling. Charlie Zonnican's *O308 Jules Denye* (named after a Belgian boat builder) was unreliable so he moved to the local pilchard boat *PZ36 Gleaner*. After the war, he built a new trawler O306; he had wanted the same name and registration but O36 was not available and the sign writer made a mistake, so she became *O306 Cleaner*! The Zeebrugge trawler *Z34 Twilight* was named after the Newlyn pilchard driver *PZ137 Twilight* in which skipper Franz Verlene had worked with his father. The Belgians Goutsmits and Christiaens were pilchard catching in Mousehole's *PZ198 We'll Try*. Andre van Craeynest worked on *PZ273 Boy George* and could navigate by the stars; he was remembered for having delivered a baby on board the boat in which he escaped from Belgium.[109] Victor Vantorre and Emil Calibut, who worked part-time for Badcock's Bakery, were also part of the four-man crew of the *PZ595 Girl Sybil*. Some men abandoned fishing and joined up. Gerard Vantorre was injured when the Belgian boats anchored in Newlyn Harbour were attacked by German aircraft; on recovery he joined the Merchant Navy,[110] as did Andre van Craeynest. Some Belgians joined the Royal Navy. There was also a great need for skilled men who could do repair work. Medard Vantorre worked on a Greek ship at Penzance when his boat *H67 Marie Therese* was commandeered; Henri Peters who came from Ostend became the shore based fitter to the Belgian fleet, having been an engineer on a cross channel ferry before the war.

107 Raymond Peake, in conversation
108 Perry 2001:37
109 Raymond Peake, in conversation
110 Barnes NA 2140

The Belgian Vice Consul

The job of settling the Belgian and French refugees in Newlyn was undertaken by a number of different people. The Mayor of Penzance, Miss D P Harvey, a retired schoolteacher who spoke fluent French played an important part, as did the honorary French Consular Agent, John Henry Matthews. For the Belgians, the most important person was Bryan Stevenson, the Belgian Vice Consul. The post had existed in Newlyn before the outbreak of war, with an office in Badcock's Block opposite the Fish Market. In fact, most of the Belgian boats that came directly to Newlyn when war broke out had used the harbour and landed their fish at Newlyn before the war. When war broke out, some boats came with their owners and their Belgian crew, but others came in boats that they worked but did not own and were supervised by the Belgian authorities in this country.

Bryan Stevenson could speak Flemish and had visited Belgium a number of times. He was highly regarded by the Belgians, being an important mediator between the Cornish and the Flemish fishermen. He helped the boat owners with their administration and fish sales; when war broke out, he helped in other matters, as when the Belgian crew of the *Boy George* shot down their own mast while firing at an enemy plane. He also worked on the domestic front and was instrumental in settling many Belgian refugees in the inadequate housing that was available to them, organising furniture and utensils and men to make essential repairs.

Right: Bryan Desmond Stevenson the Belgian Vice Consul.
Source, Linda Holmes

Home and School

Two or three years ago, the local authorities condemned scores of solid old granite cottages and built blocks of new ones. This was severely criticised by outsiders as a threat to the beauty of one of the most picturesque ports along the whole coast. The work of pulling down the houses was delayed, with the result that the council has been able to fill them with refugees. The former owners, who were offered from £5 to £15 for the sites, the actual buildings being officially considered worthless, are now asking a little drily how much rent the new occupiers will be asked to pay and who is going to get it.   *Daily Telegraph* August 18 1940

The problem of housing the influx of refugees that came to Newlyn at the beginning of the war was solved by using the empty fishermen's cottages that had been requisitioned by the local authority before the war for demolition. Some of the unpopular new council houses were also empty. The Belgians were allowed to move into this accommodation, which included the cottages at Farmer's Meadow.

Despite appeals being made in the local newspapers for spare items of furniture and cooking utensils,[111] there are many stories of families moving into almost uninhabitable cottages. When Andre van Craeynest and his family moved to Farmer's Meadow, they found broken windows, doors hanging crookedly on one hinge, and grass growing up through holes in the floorboards. Petrus Paulus Utterwulghe and his wife Savels Pharailde and their three sons, Emiel, Albert and Leon lived at No 4 Farmer's Meadow. He was the owner of *H49 De Blauwvoet* and died in Newlyn in 1941. After the war (1946), his son Emiel came with the boat to Penzance to bring back the body of his father to Heist. The unfortunate Richard Joseph Vanhove and his family had lived in the same house before moving to Brixham where he signed on the trawler *H14*, and on his first or second trip, the boat touched a sea mine and was lost with all the crew. Similarly, Norbert Bil records moving into the almost derelict No 9 Farmer's Meadow. His grandparents Frans and Mme Utterwulghe lived next door and the other cottages were occupied by some fifty or more Belgians.

Belgian families also lived in other parts of Newlyn. Ruth Richards remembers the Belgian refugees around the Parc Saundry area in houses that were vacant at the time, and her mother finding kitchen equipment for the refugees. She thought the teenage girls were very pretty and so well dressed.[112]

---

[111] Matthews NA 1371
[112] Ruth Richards, Archive Tape 1

Belgian families at Farmer's Meadow 1943. Left to right: Romanic Blommaert, Stephanie Vleitinck, Yvonne Beernaert, Maria Savels, Yvonne Dewaele, Marie Jose Beernaert, Melanie Couwyzer and Andre Vantorre. Source, Josef Couwyzer

Andre Goderis came to England from Blankenberge in 1940 on his father's trawler, *B30 Jean Andre* (named after his two sons) with his mother and brother. Raymond Peake remembers working on this boat. It had previously been called *Pentire*, and that name was cut in the transom and painted with gold leaf.[113] The Goderis family had landed at Weymouth then sailed to Brixham. They were taken to London where they remained for a month before coming to Newlyn. They lived first in a small house in Boase Street, now demolished and then in a cottage in North Fore St that later became the Smugglers Restaurant, providing themselves with furniture from second-hand shops. Ron Hogg met the Belgian Andre Goderis by chance in 2010. Andre was on holiday with his wife visiting the places he had known as a boy. He recalled sheltering under a steel table inside the house during air raids and occasionally when things became particularly bad, the family took refuge in the fields above Newlyn. Andre attended the infant school in Trewarveneth Street, and later the Board School on Chywoone Hill.[114]

The Belgian boy Robert Maeson was a friend of Raymond Peake, who lived in Carne Road with his father and two brothers during the war. Raymond came from a family of boat builders. His father and grandfather had made intricate models to discuss the shape and details of a boat with the customer before commencing work on the full sized vessel. Raymond also built model boats.

Robert Maeson became a cadet and went to the Belgian Congo. Later he married a Belgian girl and returned to England where he worked from Dover.

Right: Raymond Peake and his Belgian friend, Robert Maeson at Tolcarne c.1941. Raymond holds a model of the Dutch fishing boat *Jong Yan* that he had made four years earlier. Source, Raymond Peake

[113] Raymond Peake, in conversation
[114] Ron Hogg in conversation with Andre Goderis, June 22 2010 NA1961

Irene de Paep who came from Heist, lived first at Wherrytown and later at 1 Church Street, Newlyn. She came to England with her fisherman father, mother, three brothers and a sister of fifteen months. The family's first experience of the village was frightening as the sounding of air raid sirens coincided with the blasting at Penlee Quarry.

The children of school age attended the Board School and the Belgian School, half a day each. Irene's older brother (who joined the Merchant Navy at eighteen) made sweets, which her mother kept in a tin. The rattling of the tin at the top of the Slip by the Fisherman's Rest called the children from their play in the old harbour and greatly amused the fishermen sitting on the bench outside.

The Belgian Government decreed that Belgian children should attend a Belgian School and the English Government obliged all children to go to an English school, so schooling for refugee children was rather complicated. The Penzance Mayor, Miss D P Harvey was responsible for the refugee schools, requisitioning local church and chapel halls for the purpose. In Newlyn, she worked closely with the two men responsible for the French and Belgian refugee communities, J Harry Mathews for the French refugees and Bryan Stevenson for the Belgian refugees. Certainly, Bryan Stevenson intervened in school matters, helping some of the older children, like Marie Vantorre, who was aged fourteen, to attend the Penzance County School.

For half a day, the Belgian children had classes in one of the two rooms put aside for them underneath the Trinity Methodist Sunday School. Some of these children came from a wider geographical area than Newlyn, like Irene Dobbelaere de Groote who lived at Penzance. Mary Warren recalls joining a class at the Belgian School and being impressed by the excellent English that the Belgian children spoke. She was friends with a Belgian girl called Marie Louise Zonnican who lived in New Road.[115]

For the other half of the day, the Belgian children attended one of the English schools. Jozef Couwyzer from Farmer's Meadow went to school in Penzance. Jeannette and Simone Wouters from Ostend, who lived with their parents at Beaufort Place opposite St Peter's Church, went to Tolcarne School and loved it, remembering with affection Mr White and Miss Humphries (and hating the Belgian School). Roger Goutsmit had attended school in Wales when he first came to Britain, so when he came to Newlyn in 1942, he became known as 'the Belgian Taffy' because of his Welsh accent. He lived at 6 Parc Terrace, then Clodgy Cottage in Trewarveneth Street and attended Tolcarne School.

The school logs at the Board School suggest that teaching the Belgian refugees, particularly the older boys, was no easy matter. Mr Wright the Headteacher there complained that there were 60 boys in the top class, which gave him no time to attend to the five Belgians (September 2 1940). Six months later, he had eight Belgian boys in the top class who apparently had found their feet in the new Country sufficiently to be very noisy and disobedient. So much so in fact, that he was obliged to send the ringleader home. No doubt, the boy got a hard time at home over the incident as his father wrote to the head apologising for his son's behaviour and promising it would not happen again.

The Warrens at Lower Trembath farm had two Belgian teachers from Brussels, who taught at the Belgian School, lodging with them. Apparently, Mrs Nadel had a number of 'foreign' ways that caused raised eyebrows in Newlyn. She liked to sunbathe in the nude and the children at the farm were warned not to spy. She also pegged salted megrim on the line to dry, and Mrs Warren was embarrassed by the fish, which could be smelt by the people who used to go courting near the farm. The megrims were too small for the fishermen to sell and so they were dried, as were the more bulky Conger.[116]

The teachers were very kind to the Warren children and Mary remembers being taken with her brother on a trip to Sennen when the bus could not get up the hill and the passengers had to walk while the bus backed down to the bottom and then drove to the top empty.

In due course, the Nadels left Trembath Farm because of the long trek across wet fields that they had to make each day to get to work and moved next door to Cecil Jenkin's family in the Coombe where Mr Nadel gave French lessons to Cecil.

The Belgians were close-knit with their own language and their own religion, Roman Catholicism. At holiday time, they displayed their distinctive dress, the elderly women in black, the girls dressed smartly with collars and aprons trimmed with lace. They had their own club, which they called the Belgian Congo, at the foot of Chywoone Hill.

---

[115] Mary Warren, Archive Tape 1
[116] Raymond Peake, in conversation

The Breton Invasion

On June 18 1940, General de Gaulle made a radio broadcast from London appealing to his countrymen to join what became the Free French Movement. The local lighthouse keeper on the tiny island of Sein off Brittany heard the message on his radio and relayed it to the islanders resulting in a decision that most of the able-bodied men on the island would sail to Newlyn to join the Free French.[117] The first two boats to leave on June 24 1940 were the lighthouse tender *Valleda* and Prosper Couillandre's crabber *Rouanez ar Mor*. Two days later, three crabbers, Martin Guilcher's *Au1703 Maris Stella*, Francois Fouquet's *Rouanez ar Peoc'h,* and Pierre Couillandre's *Au1684 Corbeau des Mers* made the journey.

Boats from other French ports also came to Newlyn. The *D3377 Ma Condole* arrived at Newlyn from Douarnenez on June 20 1940; the crew were taken to the Mission where they were given cups of tea and sandwiches before moving elsewhere. On December 16 1940, the crabber *Cm 2212 Emigrant* left Camaret with fourteen escapees, including two RAF pilots, nailed into a secret compartment. Captain Theophile Duval came to Newlyn in 1940 as skipper of the Boulogne steam trawler, *B202 Notre Dame de Moutligeon.* He served on the local lifeboat during the war and his family say that there is a report in a Cornish newspaper of his rescue of a Newlyn girl in the harbour.[118] Madame Pourre remembers her voyage as a three year old in the *Esperance*. When they landed at Newlyn her shoes were forgotten, and her father had to ask the policeman guarding the boat for permission to go back aboard and find them.[119]

A number of French boats fished from Newlyn during the war, including Prosper Couillandre's *Rouanez ar Mor,* the Lorient trawler *Entente Cordiale*, the Boulogne registered long liner *Esperance,* the Morgat long liner *Reder ar Moriou*, the trawler *Alliete Jacqui*, the netter *Reine Astrid*, the mackerel drifter *D3378 La Brise* and the *Joporo* from Concarneau whose crew from Dieppe lived in Clarence Street, Penzance. Some boats were more unfortunate, like *Appel de la Mer,* which was vandalised soon after arrival and never went to sea. Some boats like Delafosse's *F747 Marcel Pierre* were commandeered by the Navy but released before the end of the war to fish out of Newlyn. This is one of the boats on which Raymond Peake worked in 1942 when it came to Newlyn from Brixham to be fitted out as a trawler. Raymond also worked on the pinnace *Corridon*, which had brought twenty-six people from Douarnenez.[120]

Right: The Delafosse family in December 1950. Source, JF Tonkin

Many young French fishermen fled France specifically to join the Free French Movement. They were checked by the Security Services at what became known as *The Patriotic School* in London. Many of the fishermen and fishing boats that stayed in Cornwall became part of the secret operations. On October 3 1942, the crabber *Gv5167 L'Audacieux* was escorted into Newlyn by the Belgian trawler *H56 Zeemeermin*. *L'Audacieux* had been involved in landing arms to the French Resistance and her crew escaped from the Gestapo in the nick of time. They spent the rest of the War living safely at Gwavas Quay, Newlyn and working for J & F Pool of Hayle. The Breton sardine pinnace *Moise* escaped from German-occupied Brittany to Newlyn in August 1943. This dangerous trip was organised by the French Résistance. Twenty-three people were aboard including a rescued American airman and a British national. They pretended to fish until dusk then headed north and they reached Newlyn in thirty-six hours. They were welcomed on the Quay but the coastguard would not allow them to leave the boat before they had been questioned and then they went their separate ways while the *Moise* lay neglected in Newlyn[121] until it was converted to a pilchard driver by George Peake & Sons, to return to France after the war.

[117] The story of their escape from France is told by John McWilliams. See John McWilliams, A Century of Friendship, St Ives Trust 2007; Escape to Cornwall, Cornish World, NA 1370; The Belgian Connection, Unknown publication, NA1419; 70th Anniversary of the Free French 2010, NA1422; Cornishman, June 15 2010, NA1992

[118] Giles Coinchein, Archive Day June 28 2010

[119] Cornishman February 25 2010

[120] Raymond Peake, in conversation

[121] 1943: L'évasion du Moise de Lanvers en Cornpouaille Bretonne a Newlyn en Cornouailles Anglaises. Translated by Red Simpson. NA2033

Secret Operations

Newlyn folk were aware of mysterious boat arrivals from France and stories of spies were rife. Cecil Jenkin, as a choirboy at St Peter's Church, heard the Vicar, Allan Wyon, deny from the pulpit that he was a spy and had been signalling to U-boats from Pendeen cliffs; an ardent pacifist he was a prime candidate for a witch-hunt.[122]

"Strictly between you r me...."

CARELESS TALK COSTS LIVES

The mysterious boats were part of the highly secret wartime espionage behind enemy lines. A number of groups were involved but the one most associated with Newlyn was the Special Operations Executive (SOE) that worked out of Newlyn under Captain Gerald Holdsworth from August until November 1940, when it transferred to Helford.

The aim of the SOE was to use agents to cause disruption behind enemy lines. Newlyn fishing boats smuggled supplies and men both into and out of France. Cornwall's tradition of smuggling was relived during the war, with 'innocent-looking fishing boats' slipping out of Newlyn Harbour '... to rendezvous with French fishermen at sea or to creep silently into isolated Breton coves.' Agents who were to work behind enemy lines were brought to Cornwall for training and were then smuggled into France. The training involved 'silent rowing and canoe work... how to walk quietly on shingle beaches and... using a map and compass... landing and re-embarking agents.'[123]

One of the men who assisted Captain Gerald Holdsworth at the beginning, and was later made a Chevalier de l'Ordre de la Coronne, in recognition of his work, was Bryan Stevenson, who was the Belgian vice-consul at Newlyn before and during the war. He was involved with arrangements for the small motor long-liner *294 St Denise Louise* to come to Newlyn for use by the Free French. Arthur Balls (skipper) with William Stevenson, Lawrie Vingoe and an unnamed Belgian brought the boat from Plymouth to Newlyn, where it was fitted out. The boat later went to Helford, the base for the Special Operations Executive. [124]

The fishing boats and crews used for clandestine operations were mainly Belgian and French. Jean Louis le Breton came to Newlyn in 1940 on *Cm 2212 Emigrant*. He worked with his sister in France. She hid a number of soldiers who had escaped from a prisoner of war camp and Jean brought them back to England in one of his clandestine rescues. He was involved in several secret operations and earned the Croix du Guerre and other medals for bravery. After the war, he was awarded Chevalier De L'Ordre Du Merite Maritime for his work as an interpreter. He married a local girl and settled in Penzance[125]

A number of people at Newlyn were involved in these operations. John Douglas Nicholls (1914-1994) was a lance corporal in the Intelligence Corps. He had an office at Newlyn harbour during the early years of the war and worked with the Free French in various clandestine operations. He was able to speak French excellently. Unfortunately, whilst on duty he had a bad motorcycle accident and was unable to continue active service. After the war he worked in the family business - Wilton & Nicholls Ltd, Ironmongers, Penzance. When in port, Breton fishermen with whom he had worked during the war would visit him. His daughter Mary, who learned French at a very young age, can recall at the age of three or four standing on the shop counter singing in French to the Breton fishermen![126]

Left: John Douglas Nicholls 1941, before his accident. Source, Mary Chown

[122] John Jenkin, ' A Schoolboy at War: Brief Reminiscences of Wartime Penzance and Newlyn 1939-1945', *Old Cornwall*, 1993
[123] Viv Acton and Derek Carter *Operation Cornwall, 1940-1944* (Landfall publications, 1994).
[124] Perry 2001:68-69
[125] *Cornishman* February 25 2010
[126] Mary Chown, by email

Standing before the Cross of Lorraine are comrades from the Special Operations Executive. From left to right: Howard Rendle, George Peake, and Pierre (back row) and Capt Wyndham (front left). Source, Raymond Peake

One of the Newlyn men who became involved was George Peake b1919 who later became French consul at Newlyn where he was known affectionately by the Bretons as Monsieur Georges. At the age of sixteen, he sailed to Camaret aboard the crabber *Rubis* and that same year is recorded as the interpreter for French poachers who had been apprehended to appear in court. George spoke Breton fluently and knew the Breton coast very well, so it is not surprising that during the war he served with distinction on the French Navy ship *le Mutin* when it conducted secret operations from the Helford River, masquerading as a tunnyman.[127]

The French Consular Agent

Yesterday two British people - Miss Dorothy Harvey and Mr John Henry Matthews - received... the decoration of the Chevalier de l' Ordre du Merite Maritime, which is rarely given to civilians. The presentation was made by the French Consul at Southampton on behalf of the French Government.

BBC Home News Bulletin, January 10 1948

When Charles Dennis Downing Matthews found this item in his father's papers, he decided to document why his father was so honoured and the story that follows is largely the result of his research. His father, John Henry 'Harry' Matthews was born at Heamoor on July 16 1895, the eldest of four children. From school, he joined the Penzance firm of *J H Bennetts, Coal Merchant, Lloyds Agent and Shipbroker* and in 44 years rose from office boy to shipping manager. In 1920, he married Mary Strick from Newlyn whose uncle was William Oats Strick who was harbour master at the time of the Newlyn riots in 1894. They came to live In Newlyn at the house Pedn Dhu in Lane Reddin Terrace. [128]

Left: Mary Strick who modelled for Stanhope Forbes. Source, DT Matthews.

Harry Matthews took over the Honorary French Consular Agency from William Bennetts, of *J H Bennetts* at the beginning of the war. In peacetime the job had involved arranging medical and hospital treatment for French fishermen or helping them find legal representation when they had been caught fishing within the three-mile limit.

Right: Mary Matthews née Strick and John Henry Matthews at Pedn Dhu in Lane Reddin Terrace, 1939. Source, DT Matthews

---

127 McWilliams 2007:65, 67
128 Handwritten biography of JH Matthews by Charles D Matthews, undated NA 1454

This changed in 1940 when great numbers of French fishermen and their families arrived in Newlyn as refugees. Harry took charge of the welfare and business interests of the refugees and in due course was responsible for all who landed between Newlyn and Brixham. Raymond Peake remembers taking the boat repair bills for work done on the French boats to Harry, who found the money to pay for them.[129]

J H Matthews visited the headquarters of the Free French in Carlton Gardens on a number of occasions and it is inconceivable that he was not involved with the clandestine operations across the channel that involved French boats. After the war Harry admitted that the French fishing boats did not always go fishing when they left the Cornish Ports. Many a nocturnal journey was made across the Channel on a dangerous mission with a Secret Service agent on board; sometimes they did not return. On one occasion a French skipper had set down an agent near his home, slipped up to his native village and was able to kiss his three sleeping children goodnight before taking off again on the equally dangerous return journey.[130]

Right: Dennis Matthews, John Henry Matthews, Mary Strick Matthews, and Harry T Matthews, 1939
Source, H T Matthews

After the war Harry and Mary Matthews were decorated by the French Government in recognition of the part they had played helping the French fishermen and the French resistance. Mary was given the Medaille Reconnaissance Française on December 23 1946. Harry received the Chevalier de L'ordre du Merite Maritime on January 8 1948 and the Medaille Reconnaissance Française one year later on April 25 1949.

Left: Certificate and below: medals. Source DT Matthews

---

[129] Raymond Peake, in conversation
[130] Evening Herald, January 10, 1948 NA1378.

Conclusion

When the war ended there were many street parties attended by all ages. Tables and chairs appeared by magic, long tablecloths were brought out and, despite rationing, people clubbed together to provide food for many mouths.

Above: Victory Party, Parc Saundry 1945. Source, JF Tonkin
Below: Victory Party, Parc Saundry 1945. Source, Pat Pilkerton

Appendix 1 Newlyn War Casualties. Compiled by Bob Harrison.

The twenty-one feet high granite war memorial in the centre of Newlyn alongside the Royal National Mission to Deep Sea Fishermen embraces the districts of Newlyn Town, Street-an-Nowan, Stable Hobba, Tredavoe and Tolcarne. The bronze plaque, in bold relief, is representative of the different units of the Navy and Army in which Newlyn men served.

IN MEMORY OF THOSE BRAVE MEN OF NEWLYN

WHO DIED FOR OUR COUNTRY AND OF ALL OTHERS

WHO FELL OR SERVED IN THE SAME CAUSE

IN THE GREAT WARS OF 1914-1918 and 1939-1945

The monument is the design of two artists, Edward Warren FSA of London and LS Merriman, a local sculptor. WH Snell and Son, Sculptors, Carvers and Granite Merchants (Founded in 1888) of Foundry House, Newlyn carried out the work. The unveiling ceremony was performed on Friday July 23 1920 by Sir Arthur Quiller Couch and Mr Matthias Dunn. There are seventy-two names associated with the Great War and their details are available from the Newlyn Archive.

The names of those who made the supreme sacrifice during the Second World War are engraved on a slate panel. However, it is slightly confusing as three of the names, due to lack of space, are listed at the bottom of the separate Great War panel while at least one casualty of the Korean War is squeezed into a space below the Second World War names. Below this panel is a small black panel with a single name - that of Flying Officer Grant, a WW2 casualty, which recently has been added.

The Second World War plaque was added to the memorial on Sunday November 7 1948. It was unveiled and dedicated by the Rev A Pearson, minister of Newlyn Centenary Methodist Church, who was assisted by the Rev AG Wyon, vicar of St Peter's, Newlyn and the Rev S Quick of Newlyn Trinity Methodist Church. Following the ceremony, the parade, led by the DCLI Cadet Bugle Band, marched through Newlyn to the Centenary Church for a service of remembrance conducted by Rev A Pearson. As well as the men's and women's sections of Newlyn British Legion, other local organisations marching were Newlyn branch RAOB, Sea Scouts, Boy Scouts and Wolf Cubs, Girl Guides and Brownies, Penzance Sea Rangers and the Duke of Cornwall's Light Infantry Army Cadets.

ROLL OF HONOUR

BALLS Arthur James. Photo on right. T/Corporal. 537877. Royal Air Force. Died of malaria while prisoner of war of the Japanese in North Borneo on Thursday April 19 1945 age 27. Son of Arthur James and Sarah Balls of 12 Chywoone Hill, Gwavas Estate. He is also listed on the Kranji War Memorial, Singapore (Column 452), Paul Church War Memorial, and on his parents' headstone in Paul Cemetery.

BLEWETT Samuel (Sam). Merchant Navy/Trinity House. THS Warden. Drowned on Sunday January 10 1943 age 31. Son of John and Mary Blewett; husband of Ruth Joan Blewett. Funeral service at the Primitive Methodist Church, Newlyn. Interred in Paul Cemetery (Grave 1072). Also listed in Penzance Book of Remembrance.

CHIFFERS George Basil (photo on left). Volunteer. 12th Cornwall (Land's End) Battalion, Home Guard. Killed on duty on Tuesday May 27 1941 aged 17 years. Son of Ethel Chiffers of Newlyn. Interred in Paul Cemetery (Grave 148). Severely injured in the leg by shrapnel from a German aircraft, which was bombing and strafing Newlyn harbour. Died in West Cornwall Hospital that night from his injuries.

CHINN Charles Leslie (Nipper). Stoker 1st Class. D/KX121003. Royal Navy. *HMS Repulse* (34). Lost at sea through enemy action on Wednesday December 10 1941. Son of Mr and Mrs T H Chinn; husband of Rosa Chinn (née Casley) of 2 Clifton Hill. Brother of

James (Jimmy) Chinn, the Cornish/South West boxing champion. Also listed on Plymouth Naval Memorial (Panel 52, column 3) and in Penzance Book of Remembrance. *HMS Repulse*, a Renown-class battleship, was sunk along with *HMS Prince of Wales* by Japanese bombers and torpedo planes on December 10 1941 off the coast of Malaya.

COTTON Frank. AB Seaman. D/JX222811. Royal Navy. *HMS Forte*. Died on Sunday January 31 1943 age 41 at the Norton Emergency Hospital, Epsom. Resident of 1 Prospect Place, Newlyn. Son of Mr and Mrs Cotton of 2 Park Road, Newlyn. Interred in Paul Cemetery (Enlarged cons. Grave 275). Also listed in Penzance Book of Remembrance. *HMS Forte* was the shore base at Falmouth, Cornwall.

EMMETT Allan Victor Desmond. Leading Seaman. D/J45986. Royal Navy. *HMS Rawalpindi.* Lost at sea through enemy action on Thursday November 23 1939 age 41. Son of William and Amelia; husband of Katie Emmett of 26 Charles Street, Newlyn. Also listed on Plymouth Naval Memorial (Panel 33, column 1), and in Penzance Book of Remembrance. *HMS Rawalpindi*, an armed merchant cruiser, conducted a heroic action against impossible odds when she engaged the German battleships *Scharnhorst* and *Gneisenau* on November 23 1939 to the SE of Iceland. The engagement lasted just 15 minutes and only 38 of the crew of 238 survived.

EVERSON William Herbert Arthur. Sergeant (Wireless Operator/Air Gunner). 1166619. Royal Air Force Volunteer Reserve. 106 Squadron, Royal Air Force. Killed on air operation on Saturday October 11 1941 aged 20. Son of Herbert and Ethel Everson of Newlyn. Interred in Reichswald Forest War Cemetery, Germany (Grave 12.E.17). Took off from RAF Coningsby, Lincolnshire and crashed at Lippramsdorf-Haltern, Germany.

FREETHY Thomas (Tommy) John. Second Engineer. LT/KX110385. Royal Naval Patrol Service. *HM Trawler Kingston Jacinth*. Lost at sea on active service on Tuesday January 12 1943 age 28. Member of Penzance Boxing Club. Son of Thomas John Freethy, who lost his life on the *SS Coath* September 13 1916, and Edith Caroline Freethy; husband of Phyllis Noreen Freethy of 4 Tolcarne Terrace, Newlyn. Also listed on Lowestoft Naval Memorial, Suffolk (Panel 12, column 2) and in Penzance Book of Remembrance. *HM Trawler Kingston Jacinth* was mined off Portsmouth, Hampshire.

GRANT Louis M Joseph. Flying Officer (Pilot). 153776. Royal Air Force Volunteer Reserve. 203 Squadron, Coastal Command, Royal Air Force. Lost on air operations on Tuesday March 20 1945 age 22. Son of an English father and Belgian mother who spent his early days living in Belgium. In 1940, with the German invasion of Belgium, the family moved to London and then, to escape the bombing, to the safety of Newlyn where they lived at 31 Boase Street. Also listed on the Singapore Memorial. The squadron was based at RAF Kankesanturai, Ceylon flying Mark VI Consolidated Liberators on anti-shipping patrols. On March 20 1945, following low-level attacks on enemy shipping at Delehleh, northern Sumatra, his Liberator crashed into the ocean off Peunasu Island, after a burst of anti-aircraft fire had exploded underneath the aircraft. Louis was the 2nd pilot and on his first operational flight. According to islanders who witnessed the crash three unnamed members of the crew made it to the shore, one of whom died on the beach while the other two were allegedly taken by Japanese soldiers to the nearby town of Banda Aceh but their fate is unknown. All are officially listed as missing in action with no known graves.

HARVEY Charles. Stoker Petty Officer. D/K13279. Royal Navy. *HMS Ardent* (H41). Lost at sea through enemy action on Saturday June 8 1940 aged 46 years. Eldest son of William John and Leah Harvey of Penville, 4 Seaview Terrace, Newlyn; husband of Katie Willard Harvey. Also listed on Plymouth Naval Memorial (Panel 40, column 2), in Penzance Book of Remembrance and on headstone in Paul Cemetery. *HMS Ardent* (an A class destroyer) was, along with her sister ship (*HMS Acasta*), escorting the aircraft carrier *HMS Glorious* when the three ships were sunk by gunfire from the German battle cruisers *Scharnhorst* and *Gneisenau*. The engagement, which took place to the west of Harstead, Norway, lasted just over two hours and there was only one survivor from the crew of *HMS Ardent*.

HARVEY Richard Chock. Gunner. 1831722. 15 'Z' Anti-aircraft Battery, Royal Artillery. Died on Monday September 24 1945 aged 36 years. Son of Arthur and Phyllis Harvey of Newlyn, Penzance; husband of Muriel Harvey of Newlyn. Interred in Paul Cemetery (Enlarged Uncons. Grave 346). Listed on Newlyn War Memorial and in Penzance Book of Remembrance.

HATCH Cecil Walton. Gunner. 1497726. 208th Battery, 70 Light Anti-aircraft Regiment, Royal Artillery. Killed in action on Friday November 19 1943 age 25. Youngest son of George and Nora Hatch of 2 Clifton Hill, Newlyn. Employee of Messrs Simpson, outfitters of Penzance. Interred Catenia War Cemetery, Sicily (II.D.38). Also listed in Penzance Book of Remembrance.

HELLIER Ernest. AB Seaman. D/J29439. Royal Navy. *HMS Rajputana* (F35). Lost at sea through enemy action on Friday April 13 1945 age 45. Son of Thomas and Sarah Hellier, husband of Aseenath May Hellier of Newlyn. Also listed on Plymouth Naval Memorial (Panel 47, column 2), and in Penzance Book of Remembrance. Ex P&O passenger ship converted to armed merchant cruiser. Sunk by German submarine U108 on April 13 1945 whilst part of the North Atlantic Escort Force.

HOARE Percy. Leading Air Fitter. FX81877. Fleet Air Arm. Died on Saturday May 12 1945 age 24 as a result of war service. Son of Abednego and Mary Hoare; husband of Winifred Betty Hoare of Penzance. Interred Penzance Cemetery (Sec. H. Block 13. Grave 14).

HODGE Samuel (Sam) Carter. Sergeant (Rear Air Gunner). 1179658. Royal Air Force Volunteer Reserve. 40 Squadron, Royal Air Force. Killed, along with all the crew, on air operations over Germany on Wednesday October 15 1941 age 27. Son of Walter and Susan Hodge; husband of Laura Hodge of Fore Street Post Office, Newlyn. Interred in Durnbach War Cemetery, Germany (2.K.3). Also listed on headstone in Paul Church New Churchyard and in Penzance Book of Remembrance. At the time of his death, the squadron was operating Wellington Mark IC bombers out of RAF Alconbury, Cambridgeshire.

HOSKING Bertie. AB Seaman. LT/SX195912. Royal Naval Patrol Service. *HM Trawler Joseph Button*. Lost at sea on active service on Tuesday October 22 1940 aged 25. Second son of James and Mabel Hosking of 7 Chywoone Place, Newlyn; husband of Mrs B Hosking; brother of Jack Hosking RAF (see below). Also listed on Lowestoft Naval Memorial (Panel 2, column 2) and in Penzance Book of Remembrance. Member of Newlyn RFC. A Castle-class Admiralty trawler launched in 1917 and sold to trade in 1919. Requisitioned in August 1939 and converted to the minesweeping role. Mined off Aldeburgh, Suffolk on October 22 1940.

HOSKING Jack. Royal Air Force. Killed on an operational flight on Sunday October 26 1941. Son of James and Mabel Hosking of 7 Chywoone Place, Newlyn; brother of Bertie Hosking RNPS (see above). Note: Not listed on Newlyn War Memorial.

HOSKING Nicholas (Nick) Ernest. Corporal. 5440308. D Company, 4th Battalion, Duke of Cornwall's Light Infantry. Killed during training on Thursday June 11 1942 aged 22 years. Son of Mrs Minnie Hosking of 4 Chywoone Hill, Newlyn. Interred in Paul Cemetery (Grave 314). Also listed in Penzance Book of Remembrance. Nicholas Hosking was a soldier in 4 DCLI (TA). Little is known of its exact movements during the early part of the war. It moved around the coast of southern Britain, carrying out anti-invasion duties where and when required. For most of the time, the Battalion was billeted in Harwich, Walton-on-the-Naze, Frinton, Colchester, Manningtree and Southampton. From the early days of the summer of 1942, as the risk of invasion declined, the 4th Battalion became a training unit, taking in recruits from the Infantry Training Centres, and turning them out as fully trained drafts destined for the field force battalions.

HOSKING William James (Jim). Photo on right. Aircraftsman 1st Class. 1158887. Royal Air Force Volunteer Reserve. Died on active service on Tuesday July 11 1944 age 24 from appendicitis. Previously wounded by shrapnel in the United Kingdom. Eldest son of William James Hosking and Elizabeth Rouffignac Hosking of 12 Chywoone Crescent, Gwavas Estate. Interred in Bari War Cemetery, Italy (XV.D.15). Also listed in Penzance Book of Remembrance.

HURR Alfred William. Sergeant Air Gunner. 1351564. Royal Air Force Volunteer Reserve. 37 Squadron, Royal Air Force. Vickers-Armstrong Wellington Mark X. Killed on air operations Tuesday April 4 1944 aged 25. Eldest son of Alfred William and Mary Ann Hurr of 8 Treneglos Terrace, Newlyn. Interred in Belgrade War Cemetery (Collective grave 7.C.1-5). The squadron was stationed at Tortorella, Italy from December 1943 until October 1945. From here, the squadron attacked targets in Italy, Yugoslavia, Hungary, Bulgaria and Albania, as well as dropping supplies to the Yugoslav partisans.

JENKIN Alexander (Alex). 2nd Engineer Officer. Merchant Navy. *SS Farfield* (Chester). Lost at sea through enemy action on Tuesday July 15 1941 age 30. Son of Mr and Mrs Alexander Jenkin of 27 Chywoone Avenue, Newlyn. Also listed on Tower Hill Memorial (Panel 48) and in Penzance Book of Remembrance. A vessel of 468 tons built at Beverley, Yorkshire in 1921, and owned by Coppack

Brothers & Co. On passage from Penmaenmawr, near Llandudno to Gloucester with a cargo of granite when attacked by enemy aircraft on July 16 1941 five miles 250 degrees from South Stack and seven miles 230 degrees from South Stack Light, Anglesey. Eight crew lost and one naval rating saved.

LEE Harry. Mentioned in Despatches. Lieutenant Skipper. Royal Naval Reserve. *HM Motor Minesweeper 1012*. Died through war service on Sunday December 30 1945 age 39 at Royal Naval Hospital, Dorset. Son of Dick Alfred and Lauria Jane Lee of Barnby, Suffolk; husband of Lily Lee of Newlyn. Interred St John the Baptist Churchyard, Barnby. Also listed in Penzance Book of Remembrance.

KITCHEN Edward. Private. 5436168. 1st Battalion, Duke of Cornwall's Light Infantry. Died of wounds on Tuesday July 14 1942 aged 30 years in Caserta Military Hospital, Naples while a prisoner of war, having been wounded at the battle of Gazala, North Africa on June 5 1942. Son of Peter and Florence Kitchen, Newlyn. Interred in Caserta War Cemetery, Naples (III.C.2). Also listed on Paul Church War Memorial and in Penzance Book of Remembrance. Edward Kitchen was a member of the 1st DCLI, which, in November 1941, moved from its peacetime location in Pakistan to Iraq. There it became part of the 10th Indian Division under Major General William Slim, which had the role of guarding the Iraq oil wells. On May 1 1942, the Battalion was ordered to Egypt, and on the following day started an epic 2,000-mile journey by motor transport over some of the most barren and desolate desert in the world. On the final approach to Bir el Harmat the stream of order, counter-order and disorder which emanated from various staffs would have been hilariously funny in retrospect, had it not ended in the tragic destruction of a fine regular battalion in a single days fighting.

LE GRICE Andrew. Lieutenant. 50798. 2nd Battalion Duke of Cornwall's Light Infantry. Killed in action on Friday May 31, 1940 age 27 at Dunkirk. Younger son of Charles Henry and Dorothy Isobel Le Grice of Trereife; husband of Joan Ann Le Grice (nee Marsden) of Chiddingford, Surrey. Also listed on Dunkirk Memorial, Nord, France (Column 60), on Madron War memorial, on the family headstone in the School Hall Churchyard, Paul and in Penzance Book of Remembrance. On May 30 and 31, the Battalion was holding part of the most easterly sector of the British defensive perimeter around Dunkirk. On the night of May 31, orders were received for the Battalion to withdraw to the beaches of La Panne (where it was originally intended that embarkation should take place). The withdrawal was to be covered by the Carrier Platoon and a platoon of C Company under Andrew Le Grice. The area was intersected by wire cattle fences, which made silent movement difficult. Andrew was the last to leave the position and as he was negotiating one such fence, he allowed the wire to twang. A German machine gun, which was doubtless set up on a fixed line covering this particular withdrawal route, immediately opened fire mortally wounding this officer. He died shortly afterwards. He was a most popular man and his death, so close to safety, came as a heavy blow to the Battalion.

MADDERN Benjamin (Ben). Photo on right. Trooper. 7960230. 2nd Northamptonshire Yeomanry, Royal Armoured Corps. Killed in action on Monday June 26 1944 age 19 in Normandy. Son of Richard and Violet Maddern of Evergreen Cottage, Newlyn. Interred in St Manvieu War Cemetery, France (IX.B.4). Also listed in Penzance Book of Remembrance.

MATTHEWS Desmond George. Private. 5445149. 4th Battalion Duke of Cornwall's Light Infantry. Previously a member of Newlyn Home Guard. Killed when German artillery shelled Dover from across the Channel on Wednesday September 16 1942 aged 19. Youngest son of William George and Mary Matthews of 14 Tolcarne Terrace, Newlyn. Interred, with military headstone, in Paul Cemetery (Grave 1). Also listed in Penzance Book of Remembrance. Prior to the outbreak of the war 4/5th DCLI was a territorial battalion but in August 1939 it was split with 4 DCLI being allocated to the western part of Cornwall and 5 DCLI the eastern part. Their operational tasks were the guarding of key points. In 1940, 4 DCLI were tasked with defending long stretches of the Sussex beaches and later that year moved to Yorkshire where they remained until February 1941. They then moved south to the St Albans area and Essex coast in a beach defence role. Early in 1942, they were receiving drafts of basically trained recruits from the Infantry Training Centres and turning them into trained soldiers before sending them to field force units.

MINARDS Alfred James. Private. 32677. Devonshire Regiment. Died on Wednesday February 23 1944 age 52. Husband of Nannie J Minards of Newlyn. Interred in Sheffield Road Cemetery (Grave 324). Also listed in Penzance Book of Remembrance.

NICHOLAS Cyril. Leading Aircraftsman. 643078. Royal Air Force Volunteer Reserve. Died on Tuesday June 17 1941 age 22. Adopted son of Joseph and Winnie Maslin of Newlyn. Interred in Sheffield Road Cemetery, Paul (Grave 515). Also listed in Penzance Book of Remembrance.

NICHOLAS William Donald. Photo on right. Ordinary Seaman. D/JX650939. Royal Navy. *HMS Albatross*. Killed in action on Friday August 11 1944 age 18 and buried at sea. Son of Charles Henry and Bessie Louisa Nicholas of 16 Chywoone Crescent, Gwavas Estate, Newlyn. Also listed on Plymouth Naval Memorial, Devon (Panel 88, Column 1), Paul Church War Memorial, in Penzance Book of Remembrance, on parent's headstone in Penzance Cemetery (Plot 9) and on grandparent's headstone (Mr and Mrs W. Cloke) in Paul Cemetery. *HMS Albatross* was a repair ship, formally RNAS seaplane carrier that was torpedoed off Normandy on August 11 1944 and deemed beyond repair.

OATS Frederick (Freddy) Charles. Sergeant (Instructor). 5440857. Oxfordshire and Buckinghamshire Light Infantry. Killed on service Tuesday July 18 1944 age 27 at the Northern Weapons Training School, Catterick Camp, Yorkshire. Son of William Frederick and Gertrude Oats of Bellevue, Marazion; husband of Carol Christianna Oats of Chywoone Crescent, Newlyn. Interred in Penzance Cemetery (Sec. F, Row B, Grave 7). Also listed on Marazion War Memorial and in Penzance Book of Remembrance.

OLDS Conrad Leslie. Trinity Service. Conrad was also an auxiliary coastguard and died when he fell over the cliff at Penlee Point, Cawsand on Friday November 6 1942 age 24. Youngest son of William Guy and Mary Olds of Paul Hill, Newlyn. Also listed in Penzance Book of Remembrance.

PEARCE Edward George Montague. Distinguished Service Medal. Chief Yeoman of Signals. D/J87403. Royal Navy. *HMS Medway* (F25). Killed through enemy action on Tuesday March 5 1940 aged 40. Son of Frederick John and Lucy Pearce; husband of Phyllis Pearce of Newlyn. Interred in Alexandria War Memorial Cemetery, Egypt (1.C.M). *HMS Medway*, a submarine depot ship, was torpedoed and sunk by German submarine U372 off Alexandria, Egypt on June 30 1942 whilst on passage to Beirut. Of the crew, 30 went down with the ship.

PENTREATH John Alistair Dudley. Lieutenant. 326384. Duke of Cornwall's Light Infantry. Attached to 2nd Battalion, Berkshire Regiment. Killed in action in Burma on Saturday April 28 1945 aged 21. Only son of Mr and Mrs R J Pentreath; husband of Mrs Mary Pentreath of 7 Roskilly Cottages, Newlyn. Listed on Rangoon Memorial, Yangon (formerly Rangoon), Myanmar (formerly Burma) (Face 13). Also listed in Penzance Book of Remembrance and on grandmother's headstone (Jessie Maud Taskis) in Sheffield Road Cemetery. In April, the 2nd Royal Berks were operating against Japanese forces in the Meiktila/Pyawbwe area of Burma. At 1530 hours on April 28 C Company, when advancing, came under heavy machine gun and grenade discharger fire from strong enemy positions. The leading platoon commander, John Pentreath, was killed and five of his men wounded in this action, which forced C Company to withdraw.

POLLARD Cyril Claude Montague. Seaman Cook. LT/JX212737. Royal Naval Patrol Service. *HM Yacht Titan*. Killed in action on Saturday November 30 1940 aged 32. Son of Captain Richard Pollard and Elizabeth Pollard of Chywoone Crescent, Newlyn; husband of Audrey Pollard of Penzance. Also listed on Lowestoft Naval Memorial (Panel 4. Column 2), in Penzance Book of Remembrance and on parent's headstone in Paul Cemetery.

POPE Gordon. Sergeant. 1157262. Royal Air Force Volunteer Reserve. 2923 Squadron, Royal Air Force Regiment. Killed in action on Monday December 18 1944 aged 23 while fighting in Kifissia, Greece. Youngest son of William James and Lily Hillman Pope of 12 Parc Terrace, Newlyn; brother of AB Seaman William Pope RN (see below). Interred in Phaleron War Cemetery, Athens (Joint grave 10.C.13-14). Also listed in Penzance Book of Remembrance.

POPE William (Billy) James. Photo on right. AB Seaman. D/JX208377. Royal Navy (*HMS President III*). *SS Stanleigh* (London). Killed at sea on active service on Friday March 14 1941 aged 32. Son of William James Pope and Lily Hillman Pope of 12 Parc Terrace, Newlyn; brother of Sgt Gordon Pope RAF Regt (see above). Interred Barrow-in-Furness Cemetery, Lancashire (Sec 5, Nonconformist. Grave 2126). Also listed in Penzance Book of Remembrance. The *SS Stanleigh*, a steamship of 1,802 tons, was requisitioned as a collier by the Admiralty from the Stanhope Steamship Co Ltd. While in convoy from Devonport to Barrow-in-Furness, she was struck by a bomb dropped from a German aircraft with the loss of 20 personnel. She limped into Liverpool Bay and then sank. *HMS President III* was the shore HQ for all naval personnel serving on Defensively Equipped Merchant Ships (DEMS).

RICHARDS Joseph Clifton. Private. 63002. 2 GHQ Transport Company Royal Army Service Corps. Lost at sea on Wednesday May 29 1940 aged 35 off Dunkirk. Born in South Africa. Worked at Penlee Quarry as an apprentice engineer; later was employed as Chief Engineer. Territorial soldier prior to the war. Son of Joseph John and Clara Richards of St Day, Cornwall; husband of Freda Richards of 96 Fore Street, Newlyn. Also listed on Dunkirk Memorial, Nord, France (Column 141), on St Day War Memorial, in Penzance Book of Remembrance and on headstone in Sheffield Road Cemetery. Photograph in Board School, Newlyn. It is believed that he was one of 600 troops, mainly RASC, that were picked up from La Panne Beach by the *PS Waverley* from 12th Minesweeping Flotilla, Harwich. Shortly afterwards the *Waverley* was attacked and bombed by German aircraft. One bomb struck her on the port quarter, passed through her bottom, leaving a hole about 6 feet in diameter. Four soldiers were killed and a number wounded. When the *Waverley* sank off the Kwint Bank Buoy many of her soldiers were left swimming or trying to keep afloat, but the numbers thinned out considerably within 15 to 20 minutes. Several ships in the area rescued around 450 but the remainder, 150, drowned. The paddle steamer *Waverley* (537 gross tons) was built in 1899 by A & J Inglis for the London North Eastern Railway and was taken into military service at the start of the war.

ROWE Thomas George Richard. Flying Officer (Pilot). Royal Air Force Volunteer Reserve. Killed on active service in a crash-landing in the Orkneys on Friday June 1 1945 aged 26. Educated at Penzance County School. Joined the Army in 1939 and served with the Gloucestershire Regiment before transferring to the RAF. Son of Mr and Mrs J Rowe of Orient View, Carne Road, Newlyn; husband of Alma June Rowe of Grangetown, Sunderland. St Olaf's Cemetery, Kirkwall, Orkney (Plot 33. Joint grave 16). Also listed in Penzance Book of Remembrance.

SAYER Charles William. AB Seaman. C/JX140578. Royal Navy. *HMS Dolphin*. Died on Sunday May 16 1943 aged 25. Son of Sydney George and Mabel Dorothy Sayer of Newlyn; husband of Evelyn Jessie Sayer of Lowestoft. Interred in Lowestoft Cemetery (Sec. J. Grave 204). Listed on Newlyn War Memorial and in Penzance Book of Remembrance. *HMS Dolphin* at Gosport, Hampshire was the Royal Navy Submarine School.

STROWGER Eric Leopold Ralph. Corporal. 637395. Royal Air Force Volunteer Reserve. Air Sea Rescue Service, Royal Air Force. Killed at Weymouth on active service on Thursday September 21 1944 age 38. Eldest son of Mr and Mrs L Strowger of 39 Chywoone Crescent, Gwavas Estate, Newlyn; husband of Jane Strowger of 1 Boase's Row, Wherrytown. Also listed in Penzance Book of Remembrance. Interred in Penzance Cemetery (Sec. J. Block 17. Grave 2).

TONKIN Reginald Charles (Charlie). Private. 5441010. 7th Battalion, Oxfordshire and Buckinghamshire Light Infantry, 167th Brigade, 56th Division. Died in Algeria on Tuesday November 30 1943 aged 27, from wounds received during the Battle of Monte Cassino, Italy, which took place over the period November 11 to 13 1943. Member of St John's Ambulance, Penzance. Son of Philip and Dorothy Tonkin of 27 Leskinnick Terrace, Penzance; husband of Ruby Elvira Tonkin of 14 Green Street, Newlyn. Interred in Dely Ibrahim War Cemetery, Algiers (4.E12). Also listed on St John's Church War Memorial and in Penzance Book of Remembrance. Monte Cassino was overlooked and dominated by Monastry Hill and this gave the Germans excellent observation from which to direct fire on any attacking force. Just below the summits were jagged razor edged spurs with steep approaches strewn with heavy boulders. In their defences, the Germans had excavated machine gun positions out of solid rock. In the first of two engagements, by bitter hand-to-hand fighting and courageous assaults up the cliff face and over large boulders, the summit of Monte Cassino was taken but after ten days, the troops had to be withdrawn due to terrible weather and the difficulties in bringing up water, food and ammunition. After reorganisation, a fresh attack, preceded by one of the heaviest concentrations of artillery fire, was made which succeeded. During the course of the battle, the Battalion suffered 3 officers and 21 soldiers killed, 3 officers and 65 soldiers wounded, and 1 officer and 26 soldiers missing.

TRAHAIR Thomas Thornton. Gunner. 1144156. 77 Field Regiment, Royal Artillery. Killed in action near Cassino, Italy on Thursday May 12 1944 age 21. Son of John Harvey and the late Ethel Ada Trahair of Parc Terrace, Paul Hill, Newlyn. Also listed on the Cassino Memorial, Italy (Panel 2), on Paul Church War Memorial, in Penzance Book of Remembrance and on headstone in Paul Cemetery.

TRAHAIR Thomas (Tommy). Photo on right. Stoker 1st Class. D/KX90586. Royal Navy. *HMS Exeter* (68). Prisoner of War at Macassar, Celebes, Netherlands East Indies. Died from a tropical illness during captivity on Thursday April 12 1945 age 26. Son of James Thomas Trahair and Janie Trahair of Newlyn; husband of Rosaline Trahair of 45 Chapel Street, Penzance. Ambon War Cemetery, Indonesia having been brought in from the European Cemetery at Makassar (Grave B73). Also listed in Penzance Book of Remembrance. *HMS Exeter*, a York class heavy cruiser, was launched in 1929. She took part in the Battle of the River Plate in December 1939. On February 28 1942, she was scuttled in the Sunda Straits off the Bawean Islands, Northwest of Surabaya having been critically damaged by Japanese naval gunfire and a torpedo during the battle of the Java Sea. Over 300 survivors who were rescued by the Japanese became prisoners of war.

TRENOWETH William Romilly. Seaman. Trinity House. *Trinity ship Vestal.* Lost his life at sea on Thursday January 11 1940 aged 19. Son of Henry (Harry) Trenoweth and Catherine Jane Trenoweth (née Boyns) of 11 Treveneth Crescent, Gwavas Estate, Newlyn. The ship was delivering provisions etc. to the Eddystone Lighthouse, which is situated on the Eddystone Rocks, 9 miles South West of Rame Head, Cornwall. A launch with eight crew was lowered but swamped by heavy seas when the engine failed. There was only one survivor. Also listed on Paul Church War Memorial, Mousehole Methodist Church War Memorial, in Penzance Book of Remembrance and on headstone in Paul Cemetery. Romilly was a temporary employee of Trinity House having only joined in the previous week.

WALLEN George Harry Verley. Petty Officer Cook. D/M39095. Royal Navy. *HMS Jaguar* (F34). Killed in action on Thursday March 26 1942 age 35. Son of George Duncan Wallen and Ellen Maria Wallen; husband of Elizabeth Anne Wallen of Newlyn. Also listed on Plymouth Naval Memorial, Devon (Panel 71. Column 3), and in Penzance Book of Remembrance. *HMS Jaguar*, a J class destroyer, was hit by two torpedoes from German submarine U-652 in the Mediterranean on March 26 1942. She caught fire and sank within a short time with the loss of 193 members of her crew.

WATERS George Lawrence. Sergeant. 1315374. Royal Air Force Volunteer Reserve. 57 Squadron, Royal Air Force. Shot down over Stettin, Poland on Thursday January 6 1944 aged 28. Interred in Poznan Old Garrison Cemetery, Poland (Collective Grave 6.C.3-12). Born at Cleveland, Ohio, USA. Son of Arthur and Elizabeth (Bessie) Beckerleg Waters of Trewarveneth Farm, Newlyn; brother of Doris Semmens of Paul. Listed on headstone in Paul Cemetery, on Paul Church War Memorial, Mousehole Methodist Church War Memorial and in Penzance Book of Remembrance. At the time of his death, the squadron was operating Lancaster Mark I and III bombers out of RAF East Kirkby, Lincolnshire.

WATERS William Thomas (Tom) de Rouffignac. Distinguished Flying Cross. Pilot Officer. Royal Air Force Volunteer Reserve. 62 Squadron, Royal Air Force. Killed in action over Singapore on Monday January 26 1942 age 24. Son of Harry and Marie de Rouffignac Waters; husband of Mary H. Waters of Newlyn. Educated at Penzance County School for Boys (now Humphrey Davy School) and Truro Cathedral School. Also listed on Kranji Memorial, Singapore (Column 413) and in Penzance Book of Remembrance. Played for both Newlyn Rugby Club and Penzance Cricket Club. He won his DFC when pilot of one of two aircraft, which attacked a convoy of a large merchantman, escorted by five destroyers, in the Borkum area of the North Sea. While taking avoiding action a wing of his aircraft struck the water tearing off the tip. Finding that his aircraft was still flying correctly he again attacked the convoy and later was able to bring his aircraft and crew safely back to base. At the time of his death, the squadron was operating Blenheim Mark I bombers out of RAF Tengah, Singapore.

WEARNE William Arthur. AB Seaman. D/JX283080. Royal Navy. *HMS Falmouth* (L34). Died on Thursday July 23 1942 age 38. Son of Arthur and Chrysida Wearne; husband of Sophia Smith Wearne of Newlyn. Also listed on Paul Church War Memorial and in Penzance Book of Remembrance. Interred in Paul Cemetery(Grave 320). *HMS Falmouth*, a Falmouth class sloop, was launched in 1932. On June 24 1940, she sunk the Italian submarine *Galvani* in the Gulf of Oman. Renamed *RNVR Calliope* in 1952 and scrapped in 1968.

WEBSTER Patrick (Pat) James Trevor. Stoker. LT/X9901S. Royal Naval Patrol Service. *HM Trawler Comet*. Lost his life at sea on Monday September 30 1940 age 28. Son of Trevor and Elizabeth Webster; husband of Susan Carter Webster of 46 Chywoone Avenue. Also listed on Lowestoft Naval Memorial, Suffolk (Panel 41) and in Penzance Book of Remembrance. The vessel was sunk by a mine off Falmouth.

WILLIAMS Kenneth. Private. 5439273. 1st Battalion, Duke of Cornwall's Light Infantry. Killed in action on Friday 5 1942 age 23 during the Battle of Gazala (The Cauldron) in Libya, North Africa. Son of Henry Cornish Williams and Beatrice Williams of 8 Treveneth Crescent, Gwavas Estate, Newlyn. Also listed on Alamein Memorial, Egypt (Column 61), Paul Church War Memorial, in Penzance Book of Remembrance and on headstone in Paul Cemetery. The Battalion, under the command of the 5th (Indian) Infantry Division, fought a somewhat confused and hard battle in the area of Bir el Harmat about 30 miles to the south west of Tobruk.

WINDSOR Frederick Roland. AB Seaman. D/JX135549. Royal Navy. *HMS Neptune* (20). Lost at sea through enemy action on Friday December 10 1941 age 26. Son of Frederick and Daisy Windsor of Newlyn. Also listed on Plymouth Naval Memorial, Devon (Panel 49. Column 1) and in Penzance Book of Remembrance. *HMS Neptune*, an Achilles class light cruiser, was sunk in heavy seas off Tripoli, North Africa on December 19 1941 by 4 mines laid by an Italian cruiser force in June of that year. There was only one survivor (Norman Walton) from the crew of 767 and he was rescued by an Italian torpedo boat 4 days later. After his release in 1943 from an Italian POW camp he served in a frigate on Russian convoys and then in the minesweeper *Rowena*. Recalled for the duration of the Korean War he finally retired as a Petty Officer and died on April 20 2005 age 84.

WORTH Desmond Thomas. Leading Seaman. D/JX151384. Royal Navy. HM Submarine *Pandora* (N42). Killed in action Wednesday April 1 1942 age 20 years. Son of Walter Williams Worth and Blanch Cortney Worth. Also listed on Plymouth Naval Memorial, Devon (Panel 64. Column 1). *HMS Pandora*, a P class submarine, was launched in 1929. She was bombed and sunk by Italian aircraft in Valetta Harbour, Malta on April 1 1942 shortly after arriving with supplies from Gibraltar. Raised in September 1943 but not repaired. Scrapped in 1945.

The following names on Newlyn War Memorial (World War 2) have yet to be positively identified and the Newlyn Archive would welcome input on them and any further information or corrections on the above biographical notes:-

ARMY. J. Abrahams.
RN. E. Edwards.
RAF. J. Eddy.
UNKNOWN. R. McGuiness.

The above information has been obtained from the National Archives, the Commonwealth War Graves Commission, The Cornishman, Morrab Library (Penzance), the National Maritime Museum (Falmouth), the DCLI Museum (Bodmin), and from relations and friends of those named.

INDEX